ISSUES THAT CONCERN YOU

Pollution

Cynthia A. Bily, *Book Editor*

GREENHAVEN PRESS
A part of Gale, Cengage Learning

GALE
CENGAGE Learning

Detroit • New York • San Francisco • New Haven, Conn • Waterville, Maine • London

GALE
CENGAGE Learning™

Christine Nasso, *Publisher*
Elizabeth Des Chenes, *Managing Editor*

© 2010 Greenhaven Press, a part of Gale, Cengage Learning

Articles in Greenhaven Press anthologies are often edited for length to meet page requirements. In addition, original titles of these works are changed to clearly present the main thesis and to explicitly indicate the author's opinion. Every effort is made to ensure that Greenhaven Press accurately reflects the original intent of the authors. Every effort has been made to trace the owners of copyrighted material.

Cover image copyright Sergey Kamshylin, 2009. Used under license from Shutterstock.com.

LIBRARY OF CONGRESS CATALOGING-IN-PUBLICATION DATA

Pollution / Cynthia A. Bily, book editor.
    p. cm. -- (Issues that concern you)
  Includes bibliographical references and index.
  ISBN 978-0-7377-4746-1 (hardcover)
  1. Pollution--Juvenile literature. 2. Environmental protection--Juvenile literature.
  I. Bily, Cynthia A.
   TD176.P648 2010
   363.7--dc22
                                                            2009047888

Printed in the United States of America
1 2 3 4 5 6 7 14 13 12 11 10

CONTENTS

"As we enter a new era filled with challenges and promise, we must protect our land, wildlife, water and air—the resources that have fueled our growth and prosperity as a Nation and enriched our lives."

—President Barack Obama, Earth Day Proclamation,
April 22, 2009

On December 22, 2008, residents near the Tennessee Valley Authority (TVA) Kingston Fossil Plant were awakened shortly after midnight when their houses suddenly shook. A retaining wall had collapsed, spilling more than a billion gallons of toxic coal ash mixed with water that had been stored in a pond at Kingston, one of the largest coal-fired power plants in the country. An area of four-hundred acres was soon buried up to six feet deep in a thick sludge, covering roads and a railroad line, knocking out power lines, and rupturing a gas line and a water main. Thousands of fish were killed as the sludge swept into the Emory River, trees were downed, and two dozen homes were damaged or destroyed. Fortunately, no people were injured immediately by the accident, but many had to evacuate their homes.

Worried environmentalists warned that coal ash sludge typically contains dangerously high levels of toxic mercury, lead, selenium, and arsenic and could lead to widespread health problems later on as the chemicals leach into the soil or wash into the water. Scientists from Duke University, who studied samples taken from the Kingston spill, reported in a January 30, 2009, news release that "exposure to radium- and arsenic-containing particulates in the ash could have severe health implications" for those who were exposed to it. The Emory River, into which some of the spilled sludge flowed, is a tributary of the Tennessee River,

An aerial photograph shows the effects of the retention pond wall collapse at the Kingston Fossil Plant. The area was covered with coal ash sludge.

the main source of water for the city of Chattanooga and for people further downstream in Tennessee as well as in Alabama and Kentucky. Tom Kilgore, president and chief executive officer of the TVA, testified before the U.S. Senate's Environment and Public Works Committee on January 8, 2009, promising, "TVA will do a first-rate job of containment and remediation of the problems caused by the spill. We are going to be able to look our neighbors in the eye and say that TVA is doing the right thing." But the cleanup has been a larger undertaking than anyone expected: By the end of June 2009, six months after the spill, less than 5 percent of the sludge had been cleaned up.

In the wake of the Kingston accident, average American citizens—who watched dramatic videos of grey sludge and dead fish on television and on YouTube—became concerned about a subject that environmentalists and energy experts had long been aware of: the various ways in which coal, a relatively cheap source of electricity, is also a serious source of pollution. The United States has some six hundred coal-fired power plants, producing about a third of the nation's electricity. After the Tennessee Valley accident, people learned that the pond filled with coal ash sludge in Tennessee was not unusual—there are hundreds of these ponds throughout the United States, and there are no federal regulations guiding how they are built or maintained. They also learned that the Kingston Fossil Plant spill was not unique. A large spill in 1967 dumped more than 100 million gallons of coal ash near the Clinch River in Virginia, and another in Pennsylvania in 2005 spilled into the Delaware River. The Kingston plant had had two small leaks in 2003 and 2006, and on January 9, 2009, just a few weeks after the larger Kingston accident, a waste storage pond at another TVA plant ruptured, spilling gypsum and other waste products into Widows Creek in northeast Alabama.

Ironically, these dangerous by-products would not exist in ponds, threatening to spill, if it were not for the federal Clean Air Act, passed in 1970, and other efforts to reduce air pollution. For decades, most of the by-products of burning coal to produce electricity went up through smokestacks and entered the atmosphere, contributing to acid rain, smog, and other forms of pollution. New technology has enabled coal-fired plants to trap toxins, including the fine particles known as fly ash, and store them on the ground in solid form or mixed with water. In trying to clean up the air, power companies had inadvertently created a new risk to soil and water.

As people in the United States—and the rest of the world—discuss ways to meet the increasing need for energy to power cars, factories, air conditioners, refrigerators, and medical equipment in a time of economic uncertainty, three themes continue to emerge: Energy sources must be affordable for citizens already struggling to pay their bills; they must be "domestic," or able to produce power without reliance on other countries that may or may not support our interests; and they must be "green," or nonpolluting. These apparently conflicting goals have contributed to a renewed focus on pollution in the twenty-first century, after a decade or more during which the most visible forms of pollution seemed to have been cleaned up, and most people did not think much about the issue. Citizens are participating with renewed vigor in discussions about how national policy should weigh the benefits of cheap electricity from coal against the potential risks of pollution.

Some, like Senator James Inhofe of Oklahoma, believe that the dangers have been exaggerated. Speaking at the January 8, 2009, Senate hearing, Inhofe warned, "I . . . hope that certain extremist groups refrain from exploiting this incident to further a political objective, namely to eradicate the use of coal in this country. We all know that would be a disaster for energy security, for jobs, and for the health of our economy." But Kate Smolski, of the environmental group Greenpeace, wrote in a December 23, 2008, news release, "This spill shows that coal can never be 'clean.'" Debate about "clean coal" has been part of a larger debate about pollution caused by other forms of energy production, by the manufacture and disposal of electronics and other consumer goods, and by the foods we eat.

These problems with pollution—and the best ways to solve them—are addressed by the authors of the viewpoints in *Issues That Concern You: Pollution*. In addition, the volume contains several appendixes to help the reader understand and explore the topic, including a thorough bibliography and a list of organizations to contact for further information. The appendix titled "What You Should Know About Pollution" offers facts about air pollution, water pollution, and electronic waste, as well as a sampling of public opinions about pollution. The appendix "What You Should Do About Pollution" offers tips for young people interested in reducing pollution in their own lives and the lives of others. With all these features, *Issues That Concern You: Pollution* provides an excellent resource for everyone interested in this issue.

ONE

Pollution Levels Are Deadly

Stephen Leahy

> In the following viewpoint Stephen Leahy describes a report issued in late 2008 by two environmental study groups, the Blacksmith Institute and Green Cross Switzerland, identifying the ten most serious pollution problems facing the world. Pollution is a widespread problem, especially in poor countries, he writes, and it is especially dangerous for women and children. Nearly 1 billion people suffer ill health effects of exposure to pollution each year, according to the report, but many of the activities that expose poor people to pollution could be avoided with better education and assistance from wealthier nations. Leahy is an independent environmental journalist who has published in national and international publications, including *New Scientist, Audubon,* and *BBC Wildlife*. He lives near Toronto, Canada, but travels around the world to report and deliver speeches on environmental issues.

Gold mining and recycling car batteries are two of the world's Top 10 most dangerous pollution problems, and the least known, according [to] a new report.

The health of hundreds of millions of people is affected and millions die because of preventable pollution problems like toxic

Stephen Leahy, "Worst Forms of Pollution Killing Millions," Inter Press Service, October 23, 2008. Reproduced by permission.

Heavy pollution is common in China. In 2008 the Blacksmith Institute named Linfen and Tianying as two of the ten most heavily polluted cities in the world.

waste, air pollution, ground and surface water contamination, metal smelting and processing, used car battery recycling and artisanal gold mining, the "Top Ten" report found.

"The global health burden from pollution is astonishing, and mainly affects women and children," said Richard Fuller, director of the New York–based Blacksmith Institute, an independent environmental group that released the list Tuesday [October 21, 2008] in partnership with Green Cross Switzerland.

"The world community needs to wake up to this fact," Fuller told IPS [Inter Press Service].

In previous years, the Blacksmith Institute has released a Top Ten list of toxic sites. The Institute continues to compile a detailed database with over 600 toxic sites and will release the world's first detailed global inventory in a couple of years.

However, this year, rather than focus on places, it wants to bring specific pollution issues to world attention. And in particular highlight the health impacts—a 2007 Cornell University study [indicates] that 40 percent of all deaths worldwide are directly attributable to pollution, he said.

Remediation and preventing much of this pollution are not only possible but cost-effective, especially when compared to other international efforts to improve health in developing countries.

Brain-Damaged Children

Sometimes it is simply a matter of information and alternatives, as Fuller learned on a recent investigation in Dakar, the capital of Senegal, where children had died from lead poisoning. "Women from some poor areas of Dakar were hoping to make some money recycling car batteries and ended up accidentally killing their children," he said.

In the tropics, car batteries only last a year or two and so there is a thriving recycling industry. However, much of this is done by very poor people who break open the batteries with axes and melt them down on open fires. Lead dust fills the air and children playing nearby inhaled the toxic lead dust, and some died.

"It is very difficult to die from lead poisoning, it takes an awful lot of lead," Fuller said.

Fuller and colleagues measured the lead levels in the blood of surviving children and found levels 10 times the maximum allowed in the U.S. Lead is a potent neurotoxin and children are especially sensitive, as it affects their developing nervous systems and brains. "These are now the brain-damaged children of Dakar," he said.

Blacksmith arranged to have the site in Dakar cleaned up but because it is an important source of income for the poor, the batteries are still collected but are now being shipped to proper recycling facilities. The World Health Organisation is trying to treat the affected children, he said.

"There is no simple, universal solution. It has to be solved on [a] step by step, one place at a time basis," Fuller noted.

Miners in Danger

Another of the biggest overlooked pollution issues comes from artisanal and small-scale mining involving some 15 million miners, including 4.5 million women and 600,000 children, the report finds. As much as 95 percent of the mercury used to recover the gold ends up in the environment. That mercury represents 30 percent of all mercury emitted into the global environment each year from all sources including power plants, according to the U.N. Industrial Development Organisation.

"It's an enormous problem that transcends boundaries. That mercury ends up in the tuna we eat here in North America," Fuller said.

Mercury is another potent neurotoxin and is dangerous in extremely small quantities. Hundreds of kilogrammes are used every day for gold recovery. "Artisanal miners are the poorest of the poor and you can't just tell them to stop," he said.

There are safer and more effective ways of recover[ing] gold using a simple tool called a "retort" but education and retraining is required. Blacksmith and its partners have had good success in teaching and then paying a leader in the community to train local miners on the safer technique.

"It doesn't take that much money to solve these pollution problems," he said.

And the pollution that affects the health of nearly a billion people and impairs countries' economy development could be fixed in just 20 to 30 years with a concerted effort by the international community. "Governments are becoming interested in this. I'm cautiously optimistic," Fuller said.

Education and other international development assistance efforts will fail without reducing the pollution burden that affects the mental and physical capacity of so many people. Even with a downturn in the global economy, the argument for cleaning up pollution is so "compelling that it will not stop countries from taking action".

"Clean air, water and soil are human rights," [Fuller] said.

Ten Most Polluted Places on Earth, 2007

In 2007 the Blacksmith Institute identified the most polluted places on earth, based on how toxic and widespread the pollution was and how many people were endangered by it.

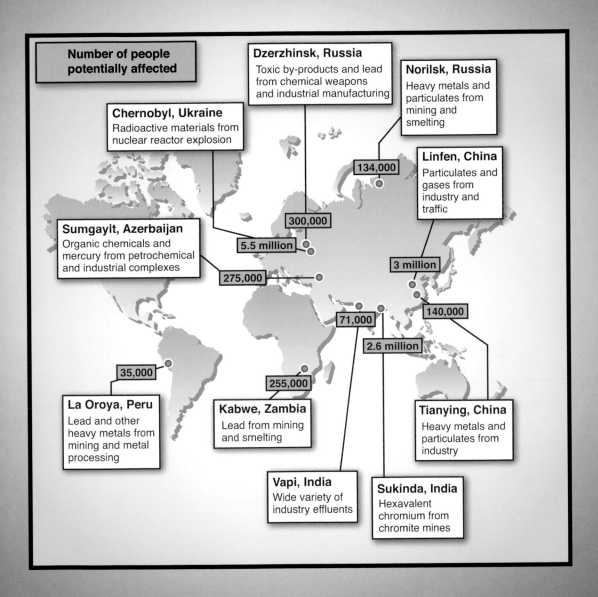

Number of people potentially affected

Dzerzhinsk, Russia
Toxic by-products and lead from chemical weapons and industrial manufacturing

Norilsk, Russia
Heavy metals and particulates from mining and smelting

Chernobyl, Ukraine
Radioactive materials from nuclear reactor explosion

Linfen, China
Particulates and gases from industry and traffic

134,000

300,000

Sumgayit, Azerbaijan
Organic chemicals and mercury from petrochemical and industrial complexes

5.5 million

3 million

275,000

71,000

140,000

2.6 million

35,000

255,000

La Oroya, Peru
Lead and other heavy metals from mining and metal processing

Kabwe, Zambia
Lead from mining and smelting

Tianying, China
Heavy metals and particulates from industry

Vapi, India
Wide variety of industry effluents

Sukinda, India
Hexavalent chromium from chromite mines

Taken from: *New Scientist*, "The World's Top 10 Most Polluted Places," September 22, 2007. www.newscientist.com/data/images/archive/2622/26223501.jpg.

The Top Ten

The World's Worst Pollution Problems list is unranked and includes:

- Indoor air pollution: adverse air conditions in indoor spaces
- Urban air quality: adverse outdoor air conditions in urban areas
- Untreated sewage: untreated waste water
- Groundwater contamination: pollution of underground water sources as a result of human activity
- Contaminated surface water: pollution of rivers or shallow dug wells mainly used for drinking and cooking
- Artisanal gold mining: small scale mining activities that use the most basic methods to extract and process minerals and metals
- Industrial mining activities: larger scale mining activities with excessive mineral wastes
- Metals smelting and other processing: extractive, industrial, and pollutant-emitting processes
- Radioactive waste and uranium mining: pollution resulting from the improper management of uranium mine tailings and nuclear waste
- Used lead acid battery recycling: smelting of batteries used in cars, trucks and back-up power supplies

TWO

Pollution Levels Have Decreased Dramatically

Jennifer Zambone and Angela Logomasini

In the following viewpoint Jennifer Zambone and Angela Logomasini argue that air and water quality, especially in the United States, have improved significantly over the last thirty years, although environmental alarmists continue to predict disaster. By several measures, they claim, emissions of harmful chemicals have decreased, largely because of new technology and local regulations—not because of federal legislation. Industries have drastically reduced the amount of pollution they discharge into streams and rivers, and illnesses caused by polluted water have all but disappeared. However, they point out, poorer countries still face problems with pollution. Zambone studies environmental health risks and air policy at the Competitive Enterprise Institute, a public interest group dedicated to free enterprise and limited government. Logomasini is the director of risk and environmental policy at the same institute.

For the past 30 years, prognosticators have predicted an imminent environmental apocalypse. Comparing actual events to the predictions reveals a different picture. . . .

Jennifer Zambone and Angela Logomasini, *The Environmental Source*, Washington, DC: Competitive Enterprise Institute, 2008. Copyright © 2008 Competitive Enterprise Institute. Reproduced by permission.

Air Quality

In the past 20 years, air quality in the United States has undergone impressive improvements:

- Between 1990 and 2002, toxic air emissions declined by 35 percent.
- According to the U.S. Environmental Protection Agency (EPA), between 1970 and 2006, gross domestic product increased by 203 percent, vehicle miles traveled increased by 177 percent, energy consumption increased by 49 percent, and the U.S. population grew by 46 percent. During the same time period, total emissions of the six principal air pollutants dropped by 54 percent.
- Nitrogen dioxide emissions decreased by 41 percent between 1980 and 2006.
- Volatile organic compound emissions decreased by 51 percent between 1980 and 2006.
- Sulfur dioxide emissions decreased by 47 percent between 1980 and 2006. . . .
- Carbon monoxide emissions decreased by 50 percent between 1980 and 2006.
- Lead emissions decreased by 96 percent between 1980 and 2006.

These changes can all be attributed to the Clean Air Act, right? Not necessarily: as Paul Portney, president of Resources for the Future notes, it is "extremely difficult to isolate the effects of regulatory policies on air quality, as distinct from the effects of other potentially important factors, because some measures of air quality were improving at an impressive rate before 1970." Indur Goklany, an analyst at the U.S. Department of the Interior, expands on this point in [his book] *Clearing the Air*. Through analysis of emissions per capita per unit of the gross national product (GNP), Goklany reveals that the cleanup of the air began well before the passage of the Clean Air Act. In fact, Goklany estimates that about 70 percent of the reduction of emissions per unit of GNP occurred before the federalization of clean air. Economic growth and new technologies, as well as state and local laws, brought about this reduction in pollution,

Through the use of its air scrubber facility, Tennessee's Cumberland Fossil Plant (pictured) substantially reduces toxic sulfur dioxide emissions.

which likely would have continued even if the federal government hadn't intervened.

Water Quality

The EPA's National Water Quality Inventory (NWQI) provides the best available data for water quality. According to the EPA report, 46 percent of the lakes and ponds sampled, 47 percent of the estuaries, and 55 percent of the streams and rivers are clean enough for any use. However, there are severe problems with these data. Unlike air quality data in the United States, water quality data lack "consistent measurement standards to enable evaluation of progress over time." The number of water bodies assessed—indeed, the estimated number of water bodies—in a state varies widely from year to year. The EPA itself admits that the data collected under its own NWQI "cannot be used to determine trends in national water quality or to compare water quality among the individual states." The U.S. Geological Survey also has complained about the deficient data and practices.

In the past 30 years, the United States has spent almost $600 billion on improving water quality, so it would be surprising if water quality hadn't improved in those decades, especially as industrial water pollution has decreased considerably since 1980. The discharge of toxic organics and metal plummeted by 99 percent and 98 percent, respectively, and the discharge of organic wastes fell by 46 percent. Just as the lack of overall data quality hamstrings a true assessment of water quality, it also obscures the evaluation of water pollution remedies.

Drinking Water

The quality of U.S. drinking water has improved dramatically since the beginning of the 20th century, thanks to technology developed by the private sector and implemented by private utilities and local governments. By the time the federal government began to regulate drinking water, the private sector and local governments had largely addressed the most serious water problems. The development of chlorination to disinfect water has particularly transformed water quality:

- As one researcher [I.H. Suffet] notes, "disinfection ranks with the discovery of antibiotics as one of the major public health accomplishments of the 20th century. In terms of risk, chlorination has allowed people to live long enough to worry about cancer."
- Since the 1880s, when local engineers and industry introduced chlorination, deaths in the United States related to waterborne causes dropped from 75 to 100 per 100,000 people to less than 0.1 deaths per 100,000 annually by 1950.

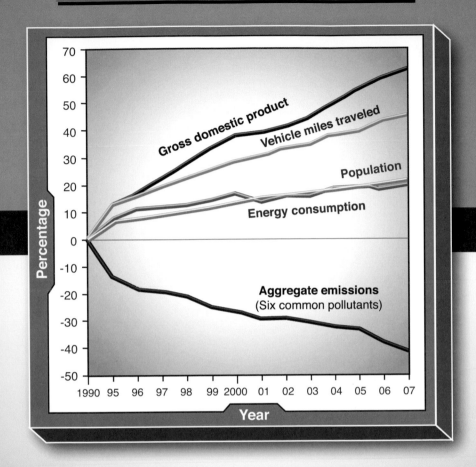

U.S. Emissions of Common Pollutants Have Decreased Since 1990

Gross domestic product

Vehicle miles traveled

Population

Energy consumption

Aggregate emissions
(Six common pollutants)

Percentage

Year

Taken from: Environmental Protection Agency, "Air Pollution," *National Air Quality—States and Trends through 2007*, issued 2008, p.5. www.epa.gov/air/airtrends/2008/report/AirPollution.pdf.

- In 1900, 25,000 people in the United States died from typhoid and cholera. Because of water disinfection programs, typhoid killed only 20 people in 1960. Today typhoid deaths in the United States are practically nonexistent.
- The inability of developing nations to afford basic sanitation and disinfection means that the quality of drinking water remains a serious environmental and public health concern in many areas. Such realities show that development and subsequent wealth creation are critical to achieving environmental goals and public health. . . .

Future Challenges

Despite these gains, legitimate environmental and human problems exist, particularly in the developing world:

- Air pollution remains a serious issue in countries where the technologies of energy production lag [behind] those of the developed world. Of particular concern is indoor air pollution. Many people in poor countries still use biomass fuels, such as wood, as the energy source in houses without adequate ventilation. Such practices have severe effects on the health of those populations.

- Unclean drinking water and inadequate sanitation also remain major problems in the developing world. Four billion children a year contract diarrhea; 2.2 million die. Estimates indicate that improved water and sanitation would reduce the number of cases of diarrhea by at least one-fourth.

THREE

Existing Coal Technology Causes Serious Air Pollution

Jonathan G. Dorn

The following viewpoint analyzes the state of coal-fired power plants in the United States. According to the author, Jonathan G. Dorn, communities around the country—and the legislators who represent them—are no longer willing to accept the air pollution and the rising costs associated with coal-fired power plants. Of some two hundred plants proposed between 2000 and 2009, nearly half have been canceled or postponed, mostly out of fear that the U.S. Environmental Protection Agency (EPA) will regulate carbon dioxide, one of the emissions from these plants, as a public health threat. Moving away from coal would be a good decision, Dorn argues, because cheaper, cleaner, and more efficient alternatives exist. Dorn, who holds a doctorate in environmental science, is a researcher at the Earth Policy Institute, an environmental organization focusing on the development of an environmentally sustainable economy.

Community opposition, legal challenges, and financial uncertainty over future carbon costs are prompting companies to rethink their plans for coal. Since the beginning of 2007, 95

Jonathan G. Dorn, "The End of an Era: Closing the Door on Building New Coal-Fired Power Plants in America," Earth Policy Institute, March 31, 2009. Copyright © 2009 Earth Policy Institute. Reproduced by permission.

proposed coal-fired power plants have been cancelled or postponed in the United States—59 in 2007, 24 in 2008, and at least 12 in the first three months of 2009. This covers nearly half of the 200 or so U.S. coal-fired power plants that have been proposed for construction since 2000. The vast majority of the remaining proposals are essentially on hold, awaiting word on whether the Environmental Protection Agency (EPA) is going to impose limits on carbon dioxide (CO_2) emissions. With further legal challenges ahead and the regulation of CO_2 imminent, 2009 may very well witness the end of new coal-fired power plants in the United States.

An April 2007 Supreme Court ruling is proving to be a seminal decision. In *Massachusetts v. EPA*, the Court ruled that the Clean Air Act gives the agency authority to regulate CO_2 emissions and that the EPA must review whether such emissions pose a threat to public health or welfare. Complying with the Court order, new EPA Administrator Lisa Jackson submitted an endangerment finding to the White House in late March 2009 indicating that human health and welfare are indeed threatened by CO_2 emissions. This finding opens the door to regulating CO_2 emissions under the Clean Air Act. Such regulation would provide a backup option for curbing emissions if Congress fails to set limits on them through legislation.

Growing Opposition

Congress, however, is under increasing pressure from grassroots activists to take on Big Coal. Encouraged by calls from former Vice President Al Gore and leading climate scientist James Hansen for civil disobedience to stop the construction of coal-fired power plants, thousands of individuals from across the United States converged on Washington, DC, on March 2, 2009, to protest the coal-burning Capitol Power Plant and to urge Congress to pass legislation to reduce carbon emissions. The rally was the largest act yet of civil disobedience against coal in the United States.

Both Senate Majority Leader Harry Reid and Speaker of the House Nancy Pelosi are strong advocates of regulating carbon

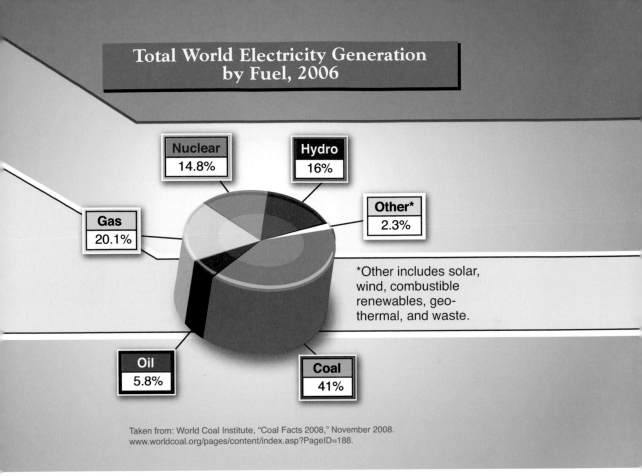

Total World Electricity Generation by Fuel, 2006

Nuclear 14.8%

Hydro 16%

Other* 2.3%

Gas 20.1%

*Other includes solar, wind, combustible renewables, geo-thermal, and waste.

Oil 5.8%

Coal 41%

Taken from: World Coal Institute, "Coal Facts 2008," November 2008. www.worldcoal.org/pages/content/index.asp?PageID=188.

emissions and are pressing to get a climate bill through Congress before the United Nations Climate Change Conference in Copenhagen in December [2009]. If limits on CO_2 emissions are imposed via a carbon tax or a cap-and-trade system, the operating cost of fossil-fuel based power plants would increase. And since the burning of coal releases more CO_2 per unit of energy than any other energy source, coal-fired power plants would be hit the hardest. With President Barack Obama calling for a cap-and-trade program to curb carbon emissions, the future for new coal-fired power plants looks tenuous at best.

Power Plants on Hold

Even if legislation to regulate carbon emissions does not materialize this year, approval of pending permits for coal-fired power plants is potentially on hold. In November 2008, prior to the endangerment finding, the EPA Environmental Appeals Board determined that the agency's regional office must consider whether to regulate CO_2 emissions before approving an air quality permit for a proposed coal-fired plant in Utah. This not only put the brakes on building the Utah plant, it set a precedent to halt the permitting process for any proposed plant until the EPA determines whether and how to regulate emissions under the Clean Air Act.

At the state level, actions within various branches of government demonstrate the growing distaste for coal. Since May 2007, the governors of Florida, Illinois, Kansas, Michigan, South Carolina, Washington, and Wisconsin have all taken action or voiced opposition to new coal-fired power plants. In her State of the State address in February 2009, Michigan Governor Jennifer Granholm called for an evaluation of "all feasible and prudent alternatives before approving new coal-fired power plants" in Michigan—placing at least five proposed coal plants on hold. Instead of investing in coal plants that would require Michigan to buy coal from Montana and Wyoming, Governor Granholm stated that money spent on improving energy efficiency and tapping renewable energy sources in Michigan would create thousands of new jobs in the state.

This viewpoint does not seem to have occurred to the Kansas legislature, which is attempting for the fourth time in a year to pass a bill that would let Sunflower Electric Power Corporation build a 1,400-megawatt coal-burning power plant in Holcomb. With vast wind resources, it makes little sense for Kansas to rely on coal, a more expensive out-of-state fuel that creates fewer jobs than wind development for a given investment. Kansas Governor Kathleen Sebelius has vetoed all attempts by the legislature to approve the coal plant. [New governor Mark Parkinson approved the plant in May 2009.]

Pollution Permits Denied

In June 2008, Georgia Superior Court Judge Thelma Moore, in accordance with the *Massachusetts v. EPA* ruling, rescinded an air pollution permit issued by the Georgia Department of Natural Resources for the proposed 1,200-megawatt Longleaf coal-fired power plant. Judge Moore's action halted construction on the plant and marked the first time that CO_2 had been cited as a factor in denying an air pollution permit. And in February 2009, Georgia legislators introduced House Bill 276 calling for an immediate moratorium on the construction of new coal-fired power plants in the state and the phase-out by mid-2016 of the burning of any coal extracted by mountaintop removal.

Many power companies such as the Texas-based TXU Corporation (pictured) have scrapped plans to construct new coal-fired plants because of the Supreme Court's 2007 ruling in Massachusetts v. EPA.

Power companies and utilities are responding to the increasing regulatory uncertainty and mounting public opposition by backing away from coal and turning to clean, renewable sources of energy, such as wind, solar, and geothermal. Dynegy Inc., a wholesale power provider serving 13 states, announced in January 2009 that it will no longer continue its joint venture with LS Power Associates, L.P., to build up to seven new coal-fired power plants. On the day that Dynegy made the announcement, its stock price rose 19 percent. Several weeks later, Arizona's largest electric utility, Arizona Public Service Co., submitted a Resource Plan to the Arizona Corporation Commission indicating that it will not build any new coal-fired power plants because the carbon risk is too high. In late February, Oklahoma Gas & Electric released a plan to turn to renewable energy and defer building any fossil-fired power plants until at least 2020.

Efficiency Is the Answer

The notion that the United States needs additional coal-fired electricity generation to meet electrical demand is misguided. Simply using electricity more efficiently could reap large energy gains. A recent study by the Rocky Mountain Institute found that if the 40 least energy-efficient states raised their electric productivity—the dollars of gross domestic product generated per kilowatt hour of electricity consumed—to the average level of the 10 most efficient states, 62 percent of coal-fired power generation in the United States could be shut down—roughly 370 coal plants.

The events of the past two years illustrate that the door is closing on the prospect of building new coal-fired power plants in the United States. While only five new coal plants, totaling 1,400 megawatts, began operation in 2008, more than 100 wind farms capable of generating 8,400 megawatts came online. Yet this is only the beginning. To have a decent chance of mitigating the potentially catastrophic effects of climate change, our attention should now turn to phasing out all coal-fired electricity generation over the next decade.

FOUR

The United States Should Not Rely on the Promise of Clean Coal

Jeff Biggers

In the viewpoint that follows, Jeff Biggers argues that references to "clean coal" are misleading and dangerous. Coal is not a clean source of energy, he claims, especially for the people who work as coal miners or for the people who live near the air or water polluted by burning coal. Strip mining, the source of some 60 percent of coal currently mined in the United States, is particularly harmful, he concludes, and the federal government must do more to protect the Appalachian communities most affected by the pollution. Biggers is a journalist and the son of a coal miner. He is the author of three books, including *Reckoning at Eagle Creek: The Secret Legacy of Coal in the Heartland* (2009).

Every time I hear our political leaders talk about "clean coal," I think about Burl, an irascible old coal miner in West Virginia. After 35 years underground, he struggled to conjure enough breath to match his storytelling verve, as if the iron hoops of a whiskey barrel had been strapped around his lungs. In 1983, during my first visit to Appalachia as a young man, Burl rolled up his pants and showed me the leg that had been mangled in a mining accident. The scars snaked down to his ankles.

Yes, but it's <u>clean</u> coal.

"My grandpa barely survived an accident in the mines in southern Illinois," I told him. "He had these blue marks and bits of coal buried in his face."

"Coal tattoo," Burl wheezed. "Don't let anyone ever tell you that coal is clean."

Politicians Have Accepted "Clean Coal"

Clean coal: Never was there an oxymoron more insidious, or more dangerous to our public health. Invoked as often by the Democratic presidential candidates as by the Republicans and by liberals and conservatives alike, this slogan has blindsided any meaningful progress toward a sustainable energy policy.

Democrats excoriated President [George W.] Bush last month [February 2008] when he released a budget calling for more—billions more—in funds to reduce carbon emissions from coal-burning power plants to create "clean coal." But hardly a hoot could be heard about his proposed cuts to more practical investments in solar energy, hydrogen fuel and home energy efficiency.

Meanwhile, leading Democrats were up in arms over the Energy Department's recent decision to abandon the $1.8 billion FutureGen project in eastern Illinois, planned as the first coal-fired plant to capture and store harmful carbon dioxide emissions. Energy Department officials, unlike politicians, had to confront the spiraling costs of this fantasy.

Orwellian language has led to Orwellian politics. With the imaginary vocabulary of "clean coal," too many Democrats and Republicans, as well as a surprising number of environmentalists, have forgotten the dirty realities of extracting coal from the earth. Pummeled by warnings that global warming is triggering the apocalypse, Americans have fallen for the ruse of futuristic science that is clean coal. And in the meantime, swaths of the country are being destroyed before our eyes.

Here's the hog-killing reality that a coal miner like Burl or my grandfather knew firsthand: No matter how "cap 'n' trade" schemes pan out in the distant future for coal-fired plants, strip mining and underground coal mining remain the dirtiest and most destructive ways of making energy.

Coal ain't clean. Coal is deadly.

The Dirty Reality

More than 104,000 miners in America have died in coal mines since 1900. Twice as many have died from black lung disease. Dangerous pollutants, including mercury, filter into our air and water. The injuries and deaths caused by overburdened coal trucks are innumerable. Yet even on the heels of a [January 2008 Department of Labor] report revealing that in the last six years the Mine Safety and Health Administration decided not to assess fines for more than 4,000 violations, Bush administration officials

Mountaintops destroyed by strip mining in West Virginia stand as mute testimony that coal strip mining is one of the dirtiest and most destructive ways to make energy.

have called for cutting mine-safety funds by 6.5 percent. Have they already forgotten the coal miners who were entombed underground in Utah [in 2007]?

Above ground, millions of acres across 36 states have been dynamited, torn and churned into bits by strip mining in the last 150 years. More than 60 percent of all coal mined in the United States today, in fact, comes from strip mines.

In the "United States of Coal," Appalachia has become the poster child for strip mining's worst [depredations], which come in the form of mountaintop removal. An estimated 750,000 to 1 million acres of hardwood forests, a thousand miles of waterways and more than 470 mountains and their surrounding communities—

an area the size of Delaware—have been erased from the southeastern mountain range in the last two decades. Thousands of tons of explosives—the equivalent of several Hiroshima atomic bombs—are set off in Appalachian communities every year.

How can anyone call this clean?

Citizens Demand Protection

When the Bush administration announced a plan [in 2007] to do away with a poorly enforced 1983 regulation that protected streams from being buried by strip-mining waste—one of the last ramparts protecting some of the nation's oldest forests and communities—tens of thousands of people wrote to the Office of Surface Mining in outrage. Citizens' groups also effectively halted the proposed construction of 59 coal-fired plants in the past year. Yet at [the March 2005] meeting of the National Governors Association, Democratic and Republican governors once again joined forces, ignored the disastrous reality of mining and championed the chimera of clean coal. Pennsylvania Gov. Ed Rendell even declared that coal states will be "back in business big time."

How much more death and destruction will it take to strip coal of this bright, shining "clean" lie?

As Burl might have said, if our country can rally to save Arctic polar bears from global warming, perhaps Congress can pass the Endangered Appalachians Act to save American miners, their children and their communities from ruin by a reckless industry.

Or at least stop talking about "clean coal."

FIVE

The EPA's Endangerment Ruling on Greenhouse Gas Emissions Is Necessary

Sierra Club

In April 2009 the U.S. Environmental Protection Agency (EPA) declared its intention to begin regulating green-house gas emissions as air pollution. In a controversial "en-dangerment ruling," the EPA found that greenhouse gases pose a danger to human health and should be limited by federal law. The following viewpoint, written by the Sierra Club, praises the EPA ruling, agreeing that greenhouse gas emissions contribute to global warming, a threat that the EPA is required to protect Americans from. The ruling will be good for the environment, for the economy, and for national security, the authors argue. The Sierra Club is the oldest and largest grassroots environmental organization in the United States, founded by John Muir in 1892.

1. What is EPA actually doing? Why is it called an "en-dangerment determination"?

EPA is declaring that carbon dioxide and other greenhouse gases are air pollutants that "may be reasonably anticipated to endanger public health and welfare," as defined under the Clean Air Act. Such a determination is necessary before EPA can begin regulating a pollutant.

The definition of a threat to "welfare" in the Clean Air Act is very broad and specifically includes both impacts on **climate and weather.** It could not be clearer that the Clean Air Act requires EPA to act based on the many serious threats posed by global warming.

Clean Air Act, Section 302(h):

All language referring to effects on welfare includes, but is not limited to, effects on **soils, water, crops, vegetation, man-made materials, animals, wildlife, weather, visibility, and climate, damage to and deterioration of property, and hazards to transportation, as well as effects on economic values and on personal comfort and well-being,** whether caused by transformation, conversion, or combination with other pollutants.

2. What is the next step? What kind of regulations will happen and when?

Under the Clean Air Act, EPA is now obliged to begin the process of regulating global warming pollution from all sources—vehicles, power plants, factories, etc. The law specifically states that EPA "shall" (i.e. must, not may) regulate dangerous pollutants once they are found to endanger public health or welfare. EPA, however, has wide discretion as to the timing, sequence, and scope of the regulatory process.

EPA is likely to begin by addressing global warming emissions from motor vehicles, which make up almost a third of America's total global warming emissions. A decision on the California clean cars waiver is due in June, and it is widely expected that EPA will either allow California and more than a dozen states to move forward with their own regulations or propose a similar national standard. The California standards calls for a 30 percent reduction in global warming emissions from new vehicles by 2016.

Regulations for power plants, factories, and other emitters are likely to come later, and certainly no sooner than at least

In 2007 California governor Arnold Schwarzenegger announced plans to implement tougher antipollution laws in California than those required by EPA standards.

12–18 months. Many factors, including pending action by Congress, will determine how and how quickly EPA moves forward with regulations for these sectors.

3. Opponents say this decision will cause schools, apartment buildings, and fast food restaurants like Dunkin' Donuts to be regulated, causing chaos. Is this true?

This is simply a dishonest scare tactic used by the U.S. Chamber of Commerce and others. While the "endangerment determination" triggers regulatory action by EPA, **nobody,** including environmentalists, is calling for regulating anything but large emitters (approximately 25,000 tons or more of CO_2 per year).

When asked about this scare tactic, EPA Administrator Lisa Jackson said: **"It's a myth that we're at a horrible fork in the road, where the EPA is going to regulate cows, Dunkin' Donuts, Pizza Huts, and baby bottles."** (http://tinyurl.com/dbc89x)

4. Opponents say this decision will severely harm the economy. Why is this a myth?

This action is part of President Obama's comprehensive clean energy jobs plan. It will help shift U.S. energy production toward cleaner, cheaper sources like the wind and the sun and spur the creation of millions of new clean energy jobs. Building the clean energy economy is the key to getting our economy back on track and reducing our dependence on oil and coal.

EPA will only issue the same kind of common sense regulations for carbon dioxide as it has for dozens of other pollutants for decades—regulations that both protect the environment and help grow the economy. In fact, the law only allows EPA to impose regulations that can be implemented on a cost-effective basis. Suggestions that these regulations will bankrupt companies and devastate the economy are merely scare tactics used by people who will say anything to protect Big Oil, Big Coal, and other polluters.

5. Shouldn't we wait for Congress to pass its own clean energy jobs and climate plan?

We believe that a combination of regulations from EPA and other agencies and a comprehensive new law passed by Congress are necessary to build the clean energy economy and tackle global warming. We and the Obama administration are working very closely with Congress to pass a strong clean energy jobs plan as soon as possible, but it's important that we don't delay action in the meantime. We lost almost a decade under the Bush administration and waiting to act on global warming is a luxury we simply can no longer afford. It is important that the Obama

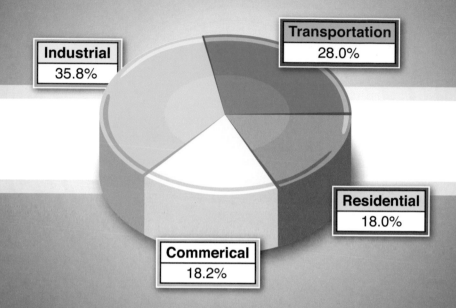

Total U.S. Greenhouse Gas Emissions in 2005

Industrial
35.8%

Transportation
28.0%

Residential
18.0%

Commerical
18.2%

Taken from: Paul Emrath and Helen Fei Liu, "Residential Greenhouse Gas Emissions," National Association of Home Builders Special Studies, April 20, 2007. www.nahb.org/generic.aspx?genericContentID=75563.

administration get started right away and this decision will allow the EPA to do so.

This decision also shows that President Obama understands the very serious threats posed by global warming, takes them seriously, and is ready to act. It also shows the international community, businesses, and others that there is no longer a question of if or even when the U.S. will begin to act on global warming.

6. Why is this decision happening now?

The Supreme Court, in its landmark April 2007 *Massachusetts v. EPA* decision, ruled that carbon dioxide and other greenhouse gases were air pollutants under the Clean Air Act, ordered EPA to determine whether they endangered public health and/or welfare, and, if so, to begin promulgating regulations for motor vehicles and other sources.

After initially promising in May 2007 to issue a new national standard for emissions from motor vehicles, the Bush administration instead chose to drag its feet, completely ignore the Supreme Court's ruling and block California and the other states from moving with their own standards.

President Obama and EPA Administrator Jackson are making good on their promises to let science and the rule of law lead. This announcement fulfills EPA's obligations under the Supreme Court's ruling. It also represents years of careful and considered analysis by the career scientists at EPA and takes tens of thousands of public comments into account.

SIX

The EPA's Endangerment Ruling Will Hurt the Economy

Alan Caruba

In the following viewpoint Alan Caruba warns that the April 2009 "endangerment ruling" by the U.S. Environmental Protection Agency (EPA) is just the latest in a series of poor decisions the agency has made. The EPA mistakenly believes that global warming poses a threat, he contends, and in trying to combat this imaginary danger, it has limited economic growth and individual freedom. The new ruling, by regulating emissions of carbon dioxide, will cripple the American automotive industry and the larger economy, he concludes. Caruba writes a daily blog called Warning Signs, and he is the author of *Right Answers: Separating Fact from Fantasy*. He lives in New Jersey and writes frequently for the conservative *Canada Free Press*.

I f the Environmental Protection Agency [EPA] were some benign government unit tucked away in the corner of some massive federal government building, we could safely conclude it was doing its job to keep the nation's air and water clean.

It is the very antithesis of that. It is a Green Gestapo that has wreaked havoc with all aspects of the nation's industrial and agricultural communities, run roughshod over property rights,

Alan Caruba, "Stop the EPA Before It Destroys America!" *Canada Free Press*, April 18, 2009. Reproduced by permission of the author.

declared puddles to be navigable waters, and removed invaluable, beneficial chemicals from use to protect the lives and property of all Americans.

In much the same way as the FBI maintains a "Ten Most Wanted" list of criminals, so does the EPA.

The EPA's former director, Carol Browner, was recently discovered to be a commissioner in Socialist International, described by Steven Milloy of JunkScience.com as "a decidedly anti-capitalistic political cause." Socialist International's principles are the communist principles set forth by Karl Marx.

Browner is presently the chief White House advisor to the President on environmental issues.

The EPA's Dangerous Power

The announcement that the EPA has declared carbon dioxide a "pollutant" and all so-called greenhouse gases a danger to human health and welfare now clears the way to regulate every single economic activity in the nation, most notably the emissions from automobiles.

Smog covers midtown Manhattan in New York. In April 2009 the EPA ruled that carbon dioxide and other greenhouse gases are harmful to the public health. The author argues that the ruling will cripple the U.S. economy.

The EPA is poised to further ruin the quintessentially American auto industry with regulatory power that will determine what kind of automobile Americans will be permitted to drive, limiting the use of internal combustion, and forcing the purchase of high cost hybrids and those run on massive batteries.

Naturally, the announcement was greeted with joy by the likes of the demented Speaker of the House, Rep. Nancy Pelosi, and a panoply of environment organizations such as the Environmental Defense Fund [EDF].

The EDF hailed the announcement saying "The U.S. is taking its first steps as a nation to confront climate change." Vickie Patton, EDF's deputy general counsel, went on to say "Global warming threatens our health, our economy, and our children's prosperity."

Global Warming a Hoax

Only there is NO global warming and there is NOTHING that the U.S. government or all the governments of all the nations of the world can do about "climate change." This is a "threat" that does not exist!

What the EPA and other elements of government can and will do is use the international "global warming" hoax to pass new laws and more regulations to destroy the economic viability of all activities that utilize energy.

Here's why CO_2 and the so-called "greenhouse" gases do not perform a "greenhouse" function. As explained by retired analytical chemist Hans Schreuder:

> With no atmosphere at all, our moon is very hot in sunshine (over 100°C) and very cold in the shade (less than minus 150°C).

> With earth receiving as good as the same amount of solar irradiation, our atmosphere thus acts as a cooling medium during the hours of sunshine and a blanket during the hours of darkness.

> Global warming, global cooling and all climate change is caused by the daily revolutions of our earth around its

own axis, throughout which time the varying amounts of heat gained during the day and similar variations of heat lost during the night make the weather what it is: ranging from plus 50°C to minus 50°C (even more extreme in places), unpredictable beyond a few days and at times violent or totally quiet.

That's quite apart from the seasonal differences caused by the annual trip around the sun and the varying distance that our planet revolves around our sun and we're not even considering even greater forces of influence.

EPA Distorts Science

Throughout its history the EPA has deliberately distorted actual science to advance its own warped "environmental" agenda. This EPA ruling permits the government to control all aspects of CO_2 emissions, short of the exhalation of CO_2 by human beings.

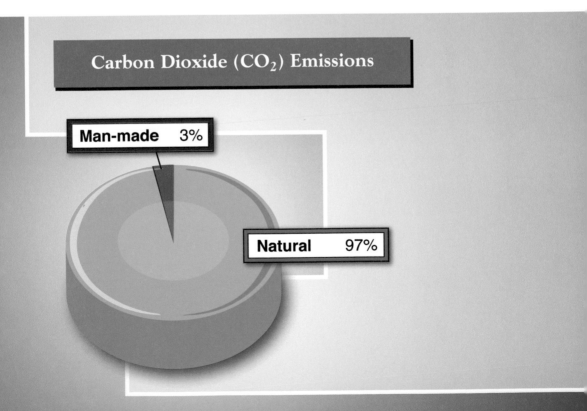

Carbon Dioxide (CO_2) Emissions

Man-made 3%

Natural 97%

Taken from: The Climate Skeptics, "Climate Change: It's the Sun, Stupid!" 2009. www.climatesceptics.com.au/climate-change.html.

Humans emit CO_2. Animals emit CO_2. And energy use emits CO_2.

It is not a "pollutant" or a threat to health; it is a natural gas vital to all life on Earth via the process of photosynthesis by all plant life. Without CO_2 all vegetation dies and with it all animal life.

Congress has a long record of restricting access to the nation's vast reserves of coal, oil and natural gas. Our "dependency," the importation of these energy sources, is entirely the result of national policies. Now add thousands of regulations on all USE of energy.

Some will mark the announcement as the beginning of the decline of the American economy, but the U.S. government has long been engaged in all manner of control over everything required for a successful economy.

What begins is the end to the abundant choices Americans have always had regarding the manufacture, distribution, and purchase of anything and everything common to our present lifestyle.

It is a cruel despotism that has been unleashed on all Americans.

SEVEN

Solar Energy Is Valuable but Not Pollution Free

Silicon Valley Toxics Coalition

The following viewpoint was originally part of a white paper, or research guide, issued by the Silicon Valley Toxics Coalition. The viewpoint argues that solar power can and should play an increasingly important role in providing energy because it is good for the environment and for the economy. While generating solar energy itself does not create harmful emissions, the authors point out, producing the photovoltaic cells that make solar energy possible creates pollution, and disposing of solar cells can also expose the planet to pollution. The solar energy industry is still new and flexible enough, the viewpoint concludes, to take steps now to reduce pollution caused by the manufacture and disposal of photovoltaic cells. The Silicon Valley Toxics Coalition is a research and advocacy group that promotes human health and environmental justice in response to the rapid growth of the high-tech industry.

Every hour, enough solar energy reaches the Earth to meet human energy needs for an entire year. Solar photovoltaic (PV) technology is widely seen as a "win-win" solution that can harness this "free energy" to address global warming, reduce U.S.

Toward a Just and Sustainable Solar Energy Industry, San Jose, CA: Silicon Valley Toxics Coalition, 2009. Reproduced by permission.

dependence on energy imports, create "green jobs," and help revitalize the U.S. economy.

Solar energy will play an essential role in meeting these challenges, but as the solar PV sector expands, little attention is being paid to the potential environmental and health costs of that rapid expansion. The most widely used solar PV panels are based on materials and processes from the microelectronics industry and have the potential to create a huge new wave of electronic waste (e-waste) at the end of their useful lives, which is estimated to be 20 to 25 years. New solar PV technologies are increasing cell efficiency and lowering costs, but many of these use extremely toxic materials or materials with unknown health and environmental risks (including new nanomaterials and processes).

With the solar PV sector still emerging, we have a limited window of opportunity to ensure that this extremely important industry is truly "clean and green," from its supply chains through product manufacturing, use, and end-of-life disposal. The solar industry has taken a leadership role in addressing the world's pressing energy and environmental challenges and will serve as a model for how other innovative "green" industries address the lifecycle impacts of their products.

In this white paper, the Silicon Valley Toxics Coalition (SVTC) provides an overview of the health and safety issues faced by the solar PV industry, including the toxic materials used in manufacturing and the potential end-of-life disposal hazards of solar PV products. The report also lays out recommendations to immediately address these problems to build a safe, sustainable, and just solar energy industry. These recommendations include:

- Reduce and eventually eliminate the use of toxic materials and develop environmentally sustainable practices.
- Ensure that solar PV manufacturers are responsible for the lifecycle impacts of their products through Extended Producer Responsibility (EPR).
- Ensure proper testing of new and emerging materials and processes based on a precautionary approach.

- Expand recycling technology and design products for easy recycling.
- Promote high-quality "green jobs" that protect worker health and safety and provide a living wage throughout the global PV industry, including supply chains and end-of-life recycling.
- Protect community health and safety throughout the global PV industry, including supply chains and recycling.

The Solar Power Industry Is Growing

The solar photovoltaic (PV) industry is at the forefront of a multibillion dollar "clean and green" technology sector that is seeking solutions to the critical environmental issues that threaten the planet. The solar PV industry has seen tremendous growth in the past decade and continues to expand even as

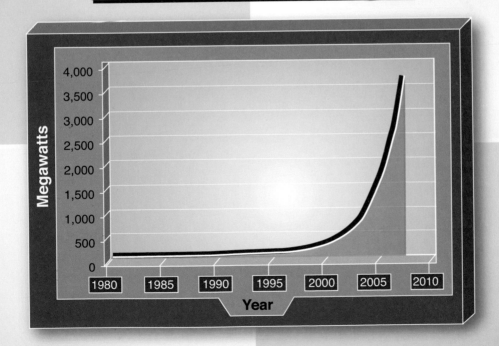

Annual Global Production of Photovoltaic Cells: 1980–2007

Taken from: Sawin, J., "Another Sunny Year for Solar Power: Annual Global Production of Photovoltaic Cells: 1980–2007," Worldwatch Institute, Vital Signs Online, www.worldwatch.org. May 8, 2008. Reproduced by permission.

credit markets contract. In 2007, the industry grew by 62 percent and earned $17.2 billion in global revenues. The number of solar cells produced globally has increased sevenfold in the past five years, and cumulative installations have increased fivefold over that time.

Although solar power now provides just 1/10th of 1 percent of U.S. energy consumption, that share is rapidly expanding as costs become more competitive with conventional energy sources. By some estimates, each time the volume of solar PV cell shipments doubles, the price falls by about 20 percent. The sector forecasts sustained growth, as calls for carbon-free energy and green jobs translate into increased investment in renewable energy, tax incentives for solar PV systems, and subsidies for solar PV research.

Solar energy is an essential part of the global move toward clean, renewable energy, and it is critical that the growing solar PV industry is itself truly safe and sustainable. Little attention is currently being paid to the potential risks and consequences of scaling up solar PV cell production. The solar PV industry must address these issues immediately, or risk repeating the mistakes made by the microelectronics industry. The electronics industry's lack of environmental planning and oversight resulted in widespread toxic chemical pollution that caused death and injury to workers and people living in nearby communities. The high-tech industry's legacy now includes the growing global tide of toxic electronic waste, or e-waste.

Disturbing Trends Emerge

Although the solar PV boom is still in its early stages, disturbing global trends are beginning to emerge. For example, much of the polysilicon feedstock material (the highly refined silicon used as the basic material for crystalline silicon PV cells) is produced in countries like China, where manufacturing costs and environmental regulatory enforcement are low. In March 2008, the *Washington Post* reported that at least one plant in China's Henan province is regularly dumping extremely toxic silicon

Solar power manufacturing in China (pictured) has caused controversy in Henan province, where companies are dumping toxic silicon tetrachloride waste, making the area uninhabitable.

tetrachloride (a corrosive and toxic waste product of polysilicon manufacturing) on nearby farmland. According to Li Xiaoping, deputy director of the Shanghai Academy of Environmental Sciences, "Crops cannot grow on this, and it is not suitable for people to live nearby." Silicon tetrachloride makes the soil too acidic for plants, causes severe irritation to living tissues, and is highly toxic when ingested or inhaled.

For more than 25 years, the Silicon Valley Toxics Coalition (SVTC) has been a leading advocate for safety and manufacturer responsibility in the electronics industry. SVTC is now applying that long experience to the solar PV industry with its Clean and Just Solar Industry initiative. The initiative's goal is to ensure that this promising new technology is as safe and sustainable as possible by promoting "cradle to cradle" product stewardship and "lifecycle thinking" throughout the solar PV supply chain.

New Policies Are Needed

SVTC is urging the adoption of policies that:

- **Reduce and eventually eliminate the use of toxic materials and develop environmentally sustainable practices.** This includes proper testing of new and emerging materials based on a precautionary approach. This approach requires that materials be proven safe before use, rather than waiting until they cause harm.
- **Ensure that solar PV manufacturers are responsible for the lifecycle impacts of their products through Extended Producer Responsibility (EPR).** Solar PV companies should take back decommissioned solar panels and recycle them responsibly. Responsible recycling does not export waste overseas or use U.S. prison labor.
- **Ensure proper testing of new and emerging materials and processes based on a precautionary approach.** Those advocating the use of new chemicals or processes must prove their safety (rather than requiring communities or workers to prove their dangers).
- **Expand recycling technology and design products for easy recycling:** Current solar PV products contain many toxic materials that should not enter the waste stream when products are decommissioned. Requiring manufacturer responsibility will provide an incentive to design

less-toxic solar PV products that are easier to recycle. It will also spur development of safe recycling technologies.

- **Promote high-quality "green jobs" that protect worker health and safety and provide a living wage throughout the global PV industry**, including supply chains, production, and recycling. Manufacturers must monitor supply chains to ensure safe and just conditions for workers.
- **Protect community health and safety throughout the global PV industry, including supply chains and end-of, life recycling.** People have the right to know what toxic materials are being used in their communities.

EIGHT

Ethanol Production Increases Air Pollution

Kenneth P. Green

> In the following viewpoint Kenneth P. Green argues that ethanol is not a clean source of energy. Contrary to popular belief, he contends, using ethanol to replace gasoline increases greenhouse gas emissions as ethanol is produced and consumed and pollutes waterways because of the huge amounts of chemical fertilizers and pesticides used to grow the corn that most ethanol is made from. Policy makers must ignore the arguments made by the influential corn lobby, he concludes, and avoid overreliance on ethanol. Green, trained as an environmental scientist, is a resident scholar at the American Enterprise Institute, a conservative think tank that studies government, politics, economics, and social welfare. He is the author of a middle school textbook, *Global Warming: Understanding the Debate* (2002).

While ethanol promoters make it sound as if ethanol is the solution to all our energy woes—dependence on foreign oil, diminishing oil stocks, the environmental consequences of energy use, the decline of the family farm, and so on—a considerable amount of research has shown that ethanol has far more peril than it does promise.

Ethanol and Greenhouse Gas Emissions

Though ethanol is often pitched as a good solution to climate change because it simply recirculates carbon in the atmosphere, there is more than one kind of greenhouse gas to consider. Ethanol, blended with gasoline, actually turns out to increase the formation of potent greenhouse gases more than gasoline does by itself. As far back as 1997, the U.S. Government Accountability Office determined that the ethanol production process produces

> relatively more nitrous oxide and other potent greenhouse gases than does gasoline. In contrast, the greenhouse gases released during the conventional gasoline fuel cycle contain relatively more of the less potent type, namely, carbon dioxide.

Last fall [2007], Paul Crutzen, a Nobel-prize-winning chemist, confirmed these findings. . . .

In June 2007, two Colorado scientists, Jan F. Kreider, an engineering professor at the University of Colorado, and Peter S. Curtiss, a Boulder-based engineering consultant, determined that carbon dioxide emissions from corn-based ethanol are worse than those of conventional gasoline and diesel fuel. They concluded that carbon emissions in the life-cycle sense are about 50 percent higher for ethanols than for traditional fossil fuels; such fuels are not the answer to global warming—they make it worse.

In February 2008, researcher Timothy Searchinger and colleagues calculated that

> "corn-based" ethanol, instead of producing a 20% savings, nearly doubles greenhouse emissions over 30 years and increases greenhouse gases for 167 years. Biofuels from switchgrass, if grown on U.S. corn lands, increase emissions by 50%.

Ethanol and Air Pollution

Although the U.S. Environmental Protection Agency (EPA) claims a net decrease in greenhouse gas emissions from using

Pictured here is a large ethanol production facility in South Dakota. The author contends that combining ethanol with gasoline produces a large increase in harmful volatile organic compounds (VOCs) emissions.

ethanol, they recognize that ethanol use is a problem for conventional air pollutants. Ethanol use, according to the EPA, will increase the emission of chemicals that lead to the production of ozone, one of the nation's most challenging local air pollutants. . . .

Increases in pollutants have also been shown at the state and local level. In 2004, the California Air Resources Board released a study that found that gasoline containing ethanol caused VOC [volatile organic compounds] emissions to increase by 45 percent when compared to gasoline containing no oxygenates. And in mid-2006, California's South Coast Air Quality Management District determined that gasoline containing 5.7 percent ethanol may add as much as seventy tons of VOCs per day into the state's air. For a sense of scale, consider that an air quality regulator in the region around Los Angeles can become employee of the month by coming up with a way of reducing emissions by one-tenth of a ton per day. More recently, Mark Z. Jacobson, a researcher at Stanford University, estimated that switching to a blend of 85 percent ethanol and 15 percent gasoline—relative to 100 percent gasoline—may increase ozone-related mortality, hospitalization, and asthma by about 9 percent in Los Angeles and 4 percent in the United States as a whole.

Ethanol and Fresh Water Consumption

What may surprise many people is how much fresh water it takes to produce ethanol. In December 2006, scientists at Sandia National Laboratory in New Mexico issued a report, *Energy Demands on Water Resources*, explaining that virtually all forms of energy production consume a lot of water. Petroleum refining, for example, consumes 1–2.5 gallons of water per gallon of refined product. Colorado scientists Kreider and Curtiss estimate that refining a gallon of corn ethanol today requires thirty-five gallons of water. But that is only the beginning. Kreider and Curtiss estimate that three times as much water is needed to grow the corn that yields a gallon of ethanol. That brings the tally to 140 gallons of water per gallon of corn ethanol produced. If their calculation is correct, the 5.4 million gallons of corn ethanol used in America in 2006 required the use of 760 million gallons of fresh water.

And things do not look much better for ethanol made from cellulose crops, such as switch grass. Kreider and Curtiss estimate that switch grass would require between 146 and 149 gallons of water per gallon of ethanol produced from cellulose, depending on the scale of production. Thus, meeting the [George W.] Bush administration's target of 35 billion gallons of renewable and alternative fuels production in the United States by 2017 with cellulosic ethanol would require about 5 trillion gallons of water per year. That is a bit more than the average annual flow of the Colorado River, which the Southern Nevada Water Authority lists at 15 million acre-feet, or a little under 5 trillion gallons.

Ethanol and Water Pollution

In *Water Implications of Biofuels Production in the United States*, the National Academy of Sciences (NAS) points out that if the United States continues to expand corn-based ethanol production without new environmental protection policies, "the increase in harm to water quality could be considerable." Corn, according to the NAS, requires more fertilizers and pesticides than other food or biofuel crops. Pesticide contamination is highest in the corn belt, and nitrogen fertilizer runoff from corn already has the highest agricultural impact on the Mississippi River. In short, more corn raised for ethanol means more fertilizers, pesticides, and herbicides in waterways; more low-oxygen "dead zones" from fertilizer runoff; and more local shortages in water for drinking and irrigation.

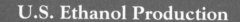

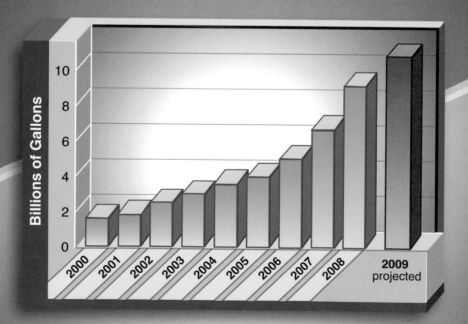

Taken from: Renewable Fuels Association (RFA), "Historic U.S. Fuel Ethanol Production," 2009. www.ethanolrfa.org/industry/statistics/#A.

Fertilizer runoff does not just pollute local waters; it creates other far-reaching environmental problems. Each summer, the loading of nitrogen fertilizers from the Mississippi via the corn belt hits the Gulf of Mexico, creating a large dead zone—a region of oxygen-deprived waters unable to support sea life that extends for more than ten thousand square kilometers. The same phenomenon occurs in the Chesapeake Bay, in some summers affecting most of the waters in the mainstem bay. A recent study by researchers at the University of British Columbia shows that if the United States were to meet its proposed ethanol production goals—15–36 billion gallons of corn and cellulosic ethanol by 2022—nitrogen flows to the Gulf of Mexico would increase by 10–34 percent. . . .

There is little question that high gasoline and oil prices are harmful to the national economy and the personal economies of individual Americans. But putting our hope in ethanol (whether from corn, switch grass, or other cellulosic crops) is not a rational policy response, however attractive it is to the corn lobby.

NINE

Electronic Waste Leads to Dangerous Pollution

Chris Carroll

In the following viewpoint journalist Chris Carroll describes the dangerous conditions facing workers in poor countries—many of them children—who make their living recycling discarded televisions, computers, and cell phones. These discarded electronics, sometimes called e-waste, contain valuable metals that can be sold, but they also contain harmful materials that threaten the lives of the untrained workers who take electronics apart with their bare hands. Wealthier nations like the United States often find that it is cheaper to ship electronics overseas than to recycle them safely at home. This carelessness, Carroll argues, could come back to haunt Americans if contaminants end up in products they purchase from other countries. Carroll is a staff writer for *National Geographic* magazine.

June is the wet season in Ghana, but here in Accra, the capital, the morning rain has ceased. As the sun heats the humid air, pillars of black smoke begin to rise above the vast Agbogbloshie Market. I follow one plume toward its source, past lettuce and plantain vendors, past stalls of used tires, and through a clanging scrap market where hunched men bash on old alternators and engine blocks. Soon the muddy track is flanked by piles of old TVs, gutted computer cases, and smashed monitors heaped ten feet (three meters) high. Beyond lies a field of fine ash speckled with glints of amber and green—the sharp broken bits of circuit boards. I can see now that the smoke issues not from one fire, but from many small blazes. Dozens of indistinct figures move among the acrid haze, some stirring flames with sticks, others carrying armfuls of brightly colored computer wire. Most are children.

Choking, I pull my shirt over my nose and approach a boy of about 15, his thin frame wreathed in smoke. Karim says he has been tending such fires for two years. He pokes at one meditatively, and then his top half disappears as he bends into the billowing soot. He hoists a tangle of copper wire off the old tire he's using for fuel and douses the hissing mass in a puddle. With the flame retardant insulation burned away—a process that has released a bouquet of carcinogens and other toxics—the wire may fetch a dollar from a scrap-metal buyer.

Speed, Not Safety

Another day in the market, on a similar ash heap above an inlet that flushes to the Atlantic after a downpour, Israel Mensah, an incongruously stylish young man of about 20, adjusts his designer glasses and explains how he makes his living. Each day scrap sellers bring loads of old electronics—from where he doesn't know. Mensah and his partners—friends and family, including two shoeless boys raptly listening to us talk—buy a few computers or TVs. They break copper yokes off picture tubes, littering the ground with shards containing lead, a neurotoxin, and cadmium, a carcinogen that damages lungs and kidneys. They strip resalable parts such as drives and memory chips. Then they rip out wiring and burn the plastic. He sells copper stripped from one scrap load to buy another. The key to making money is speed, not safety. "The gas goes to your nose and you feel something in your head," Mensah says, knocking his fist against the back of his skull for effect. "Then you get sick in your head and

A worker wades through e-waste in a recycling plant in India. The United States exports such waste to foreign countries to be processed.

your chest." Nearby, hulls of broken monitors float in the lagoon. Tomorrow the rain will wash them into the ocean.

People have always been proficient at making trash. Future archaeologists will note that at the tail end of the 20th century, a new, noxious kind of clutter exploded across the landscape: the digital detritus that has come to be called e-waste. . . .

All told, the EPA [Environmental Protection Agency] estimates that in the U.S. [in 2005], between 1.5 and 1.9 million tons of computers, TVs, VCRs, monitors, cell phones, and other equipment were discarded. If all sources of electronic waste are tallied, it could total 50 million tons a year worldwide, according to the UN Environment Programme.

So what happens to all this junk? . . .

An Electronic Graveyard

Asia is the center of much of the world's high-tech manufacturing, and it is here the devices often return when they die. China in particular has long been the world's electronics graveyard. With explosive growth in its manufacturing sector fueling demand, China's ports have become conduits for recyclable scrap of every sort: steel, aluminum, plastic, even paper. By the mid-1980s, electronic waste began freely pouring into China as well, carrying the lucrative promise of the precious metals embedded in circuit boards. . . .

High-tech scrap "imports here started in the 1990s and reached a peak in 2003," says a high school teacher whose students tested the environment around Taizhou [a city south of Shanghai] for toxics from e-waste. He requested anonymity from fear of local recyclers angry about the drop in business. "It has been falling since 2005 and now is hard to find."

Today the salvagers operate in the shadows. Inside the open door of a house in a hillside village, a homeowner uses pliers to rip microchips and metal parts off a computer motherboard. A buyer will burn these pieces to recover copper. The man won't reveal his name. "This business is illegal," he admits, offering a cigarette. In the same village, several men huddle inside a shed, heating circuit boards over a flame to extract metal. Outside the door lies a pile of scorched boards. In another village a few miles away, a woman stacks up bags of circuit boards in her house. She shoos my translator and me away. Continuing through the hills, I see people tearing apart car batteries, alternators, and high-voltage cable for recycling, and others hauling aluminum scrap to an aging smelter. But I find no one else working with electronics. In Taizhou, at least, the e-waste business seems to be waning.

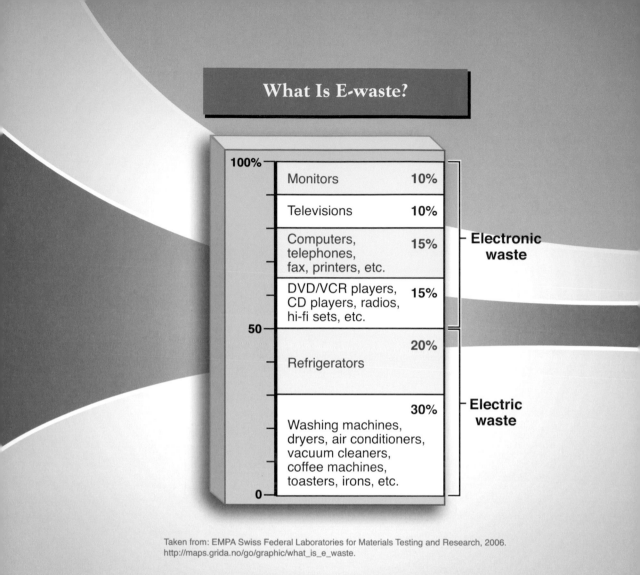

What Is E-waste?

Monitors	10%
Televisions	10%
Computers, telephones, fax, printers, etc.	15%
DVD/VCR players, CD players, radios, hi-fi sets, etc.	15%
Refrigerators	20%
Washing machines, dryers, air conditioners, vacuum cleaners, coffee machines, toasters, irons, etc.	30%

Electronic waste

Electric waste

Taken from: EMPA Swiss Federal Laboratories for Materials Testing and Research, 2006.
http://maps.grida.no/go/graphic/what_is_e_waste.

Yet for some people it is likely too late; a cycle of disease or disability is already in motion. . . . The air near some electronics salvage operations that remain open contains the highest amounts of dioxin measured anywhere in the world. Soils are saturated with the chemical, a probable carcinogen that may disrupt endocrine and immune function. High levels of flame retardants called PBDEs—common in electronics, and potentially damaging to fetal development even at very low levels— turned up in the blood of the electronics workers. The high school teacher in Taizhou says his students found high levels of

PBDEs in plants and animals. Humans were also tested, but he was not at liberty to discuss the results.

Coming Full Circle

China may someday succeed in curtailing electronic waste imports. But e-waste flows like water. Shipments that a few years ago might have gone to ports in Guangdong or Zhejiang Provinces can easily be diverted to friendlier environs in Thailand, Pakistan, or elsewhere. "It doesn't help in a global sense for one place like China, or India, to become restrictive," says David N. Pellow, an ethnic studies professor at the University of California, San Diego, who studies electronic waste from a social justice perspective. "The flow simply shifts as it takes the path of least resistance to the bottom." . . .

Ultimately, shipping e-waste overseas may be no bargain even for the developed world. In 2006, Jeffrey Weidenhamer, a chemist at Ashland University in Ohio, bought some cheap, Chinese-made jewelry at a local dollar store for his class to analyze. That the jewelry contained high amounts of lead was distressing, but hardly a surprise; Chinese-made leaded jewelry is all too commonly marketed in the U.S. More revealing were the amounts of copper and tin alloyed with the lead. As Weidenhamer and his colleague Michael Clement argued in a scientific paper published this past July [2007], the proportions of these metals in some samples suggest their source was leaded solder used in the manufacture of electronic circuit boards.

"The U.S. right now is shipping large quantities of leaded materials to China, and China is the world's major manufacturing center," Weidenhamer says. "It's not all that surprising things are coming full circle and now we're getting contaminated products back." In a global economy, out of sight will not stay out of mind for long.

TEN

Eating Meat
Causes Pollution

Kathy Freston

In the following viewpoint Kathy Freston argues that eating meat is a significant cause of pollution, because raising animals for consumption requires large amounts of fertilizer and other chemicals and because the animals themselves generate contaminated waste. Specifically, she addresses those who believe that eating chicken is a good environmental choice, contending that, by several measures, chickens are just as polluting as other meat sources. The best way to reduce the amount of diet-caused pollution, she concludes, is to reduce or eliminate meat from one's diet. Freston is a health and wellness expert who writes frequently about nutrition, vegetarianism, and the environment. Her books include *Quantum Wellness: A Practical and Spiritual Guide to Health and Happiness*.

[An April 2009 *New York Times* column by] Nicholas Kristof discusses the recent work by animal activists on behalf of chickens and pigs, and the degree to which "animal rights are now firmly on the mainstream ethical agenda" in the United States, as they have been for some years in Europe. I am delighted to see from Mr. Kristof yet another thoughtful essay

Kathy Freston, "Red Meat or Chicken? Why It's Wise to Stay Away from Both," AlterNet, April 16, 2009. Reproduced by permission.

about a moral issue that is, until recently, not widely discussed, and even more pleased that in discussing the cruelties of modern intensive farms, he is focusing on birds.

You see, people often tell me that they've given up eating red meat out of concern for animals, the environment, or their health (or all three). Of course all efforts to make the world a kinder and less polluted place should be applauded. But here's the thing: cutting out red meat while still eating chicken doesn't address the whole problem.

Here's why: Both choices—beef and chicken—badly damage the environment, so choosing one or the other is sort of like the difference between driving a huge SUV and a Hummer. That's also why I'm a little baffled when some environmental organizations say that cutting out beef is advisable, but eating other meats is "relatively" ok. It's really not.

Global Warming and Meat Eating

On the issue of global warming, all animal agriculture is a nightmare, relative to producing grains and beans. In a 400 page report from the United Nation's Food and Agricultural Organization, *Livestock's Long Shadow*, scientists conclude that the business of raising animals for food is responsible for about 18 percent of all warming—in fact meat causes about 40 percent more warming than all cars, trucks, and planes combined.

That is in part because turning animals into meat requires many stages of (energy intensive and polluting) production (i.e., transporting feed, animals, and meat; running feed mills, factory farms, and slaughterhouses; refrigerating carcasses during transport and in grocery stores—chickens are at least as energy consumptive as cattle for all these stages), compared to plant foods.

Environmental Defense calculated that if every American skipped one meal of chicken per week and substituted vegetarian foods instead, the carbon dioxide savings would be the same as taking more than half a million cars off of U.S. roads. Imaging if we dropped all meat from our diets altogether.

In an extensive report the United Nations determined that raising animals for food causes about 18 percent of all global warming.

Polluted Manure

And it's not just global warming, of course: In a story about chicken waste pollution, the *New York Times* reported in November [2008] that "[a]lthough the dairy and hog industry in states near the bay produce more pounds of manure, poultry waste has more than twice the concentration of pollutants per pound." I assume that's in part because poultry are given a lot more drugs than pigs and cattle—because they're kept in even worse conditions and thus require more drugs.

When you have the attorney general of a state like Oklahoma battling poultry producers over the industry "wreak[ing] havoc in the 1-million-acre Illinois River watershed, turning it into a murky, sludgy mess," it seems pretty clear (to me) that environmentalists might want to think again about putting that product into even a "relatively" favorable category.

So it makes more sense to cut down on meat altogether, in favor of a more plant based diet, rather than trying to sort out which meats are relatively better or worse. And we can do so in stages.

Reducing Meat Consumption Gradually

For example, after looking at the health and environmental problems associated with chicken, beef, and pork, *New York Times* food writer Mark Bittman (in his superb new book *Food Matters*) suggests eating exclusively plant-based foods until 6 P.M., and then eating whatever you want for dinner. I know people who have tried this sort of plan, and they find—quickly—that they're eating more and more vegetarian food, even during the times when they eat whatever they want. Writes Bittman, "By reducing the amount of meat we eat, we can grow and kill fewer animals. That means less environmental damage, including climate change; fewer antibiotics in the water and food supplies; fewer pesticides and herbicides; reduced cruelty; and so on. It also means better health for you."

Similarly, the Johns Hopkins Bloomberg School of Health leads the "Meatless Mondays" campaign, which is supported by 28 other public health schools. Their goal is to cut Americans'

Meat as a Source of Greenhouse Gas

Worldwide, raising lifestock for human consumption is the second largest source of greenhouse gas emissions.

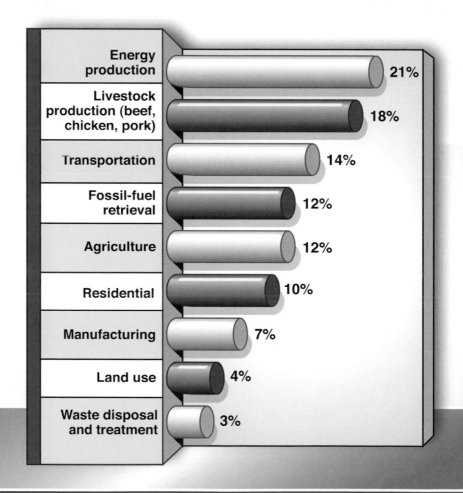

Energy production	21%
Livestock production (beef, chicken, pork)	18%
Transportation	14%
Fossil-fuel retrieval	12%
Agriculture	12%
Residential	10%
Manufacturing	7%
Land use	4%
Waste disposal and treatment	3%

Total is greater than 100% because of rounding

meat consumption, in order to lessen our risk for heart disease, cancer, diabetes, obesity, and so on. And of course, they rightly impugn all meat, not just "red" meat.

Although he vigorously advocates vegetarianism, the much adored Buddhist monk and Zen master, Thich Nhat Hanh, writes in his latest book that "[i]f you're not able to entirely stop eating meat, you can still decide to make an effort to cut back. By cutting meat out of your diet ten or even five days a month, you will already be performing a miracle—a miracle that will help solve the problem of hunger in the developing world and dramatically reduce greenhouse gases."

These suggestions from Bittman, Johns Hopkins, and Thich Nhat Hanh strike me as much better half-measure alternatives to picking between various meats.

Chicken No Better than Red Meat

For those who want to do well by the environment, have more robust health, and consider the welfare of animals, the solution is not to just give up eating red meat, but rather lean away from eating animal products—chicken included—altogether.

A few things to remember:

- for animals the poultry industry is much worse than the beef or pork industries;
- for your health, it's a toss up at best;
- and for the environment, the poultry industry may not be quite as bad on global warming, but it's still bad, and it appears to be even worse in categories like water and air pollution.

ELEVEN

New Regulations Are Needed to Reduce Water Pollution

Craig Cox

In the following viewpoint Craig Cox describes the "dead zone" that is forming in the Gulf of Mexico, largely as a result of agricultural pollution generated along the Mississippi River. He argues that farmers and ranchers need to change some of their practices so that less soil, fertilizer, and manure is washed into rivers and streams. Scientists understand rather well what needs to be done, he concludes, but only laws and regulations will force farmers and ranchers to make the necessary changes. Cox is a member of the Environmental Working Group, directing the organization's research and advocacy work in agriculture, renewable energy, and climate change. He has degrees in wildlife ecology and agricultural economics.

Nitrogen and phosphorus pollution flowing from the Mississippi River is devastating the northern Gulf of Mexico and impacting human health, killing fish and limiting recreation along the way. Each summer, this pollution causes a "Dead Zone" to form in the Gulf where too little oxygen is present to support sea life. Since 1985, when regular measurements were first taken of the dead zone, it has continued to grow. This year

Craig Cox, "Pollution Solutions for Gulf 'Dead Zone' Disaster," Environmental Working Group, October 17, 2008. Reproduced by permission.

[2008], it grew to 8,000 square miles, its second largest measurement to date.

Scientists from the U.S. Geological Survey reported in February 2008 that agricultural sources account for 70 percent of the nitrogen and phosphorus delivered to the Dead Zone. They found that just nine states—including Iowa—contribute 75 percent of nitrogen and phosphorus. These nine states account for only about one-third of the Mississippi drainage area yet are the source of three-quarters of the nutrients, mostly from agriculture.

The Dead Zone in the Gulf of Mexico may seem far away from where we live in Iowa, but the nitrogen and phosphorus pollution that cause the Dead Zone in the Gulf also cause serious problems in Iowa waters, including frequent algae blooms,

This NASA satellite picture of the coasts of Louisiana and Texas shows the polluting effects of nitrogen and phosphorus runoff from the Mississippi River that contribute to an eight-thousand-mile "dead zone" in the Gulf of Mexico.

low oxygen levels and threats to drinking water. Iowa rivers and lakes have some of the highest nitrogen and phosphorus pollution levels when compared to other regions of the country and the world. Our state list of impaired waters identifies nitrogen and phosphorus pollution as a cause of the impairment for 32 lakes and 33 river segments in the state.

Seeking solutions to stem our agricultural pollution will help our neighbors downstream and improve water quality here at home.

A New Approach to Conservation

Scientists and conservationists in Iowa—and across the nation—who study the problem have recommended that a three-pronged approach be taken. First we need to keep the soil in place and build its capacity to hold onto nutrients and water. Second, farmers and ranchers need to better manage nitrogen and phosphorus applied to agricultural fields in fertilizers and manures. Management plans must ensure that most of that nitrogen and phosphorus stays in soil or gets taken up by crops, rather than running off or leaching into lakes, rivers, streams and groundwater. Finally, we need to increase the amount of nitrogen, phosphorus and sediment that is captured in wetlands, filter strips [areas of vegetation often planted between cropland and bodies of water to filter out sediment, manure, and other harmful elements], riparian zones [areas of trees and other plants around a body of water that act as filters and prevent erosion] and in stream channels themselves.

There are proven conservation practices and systems that address the recommendations outlined above, but not enough farmers employ them. To encourage their use, we rely almost exclusively on voluntary, federally- and state-funded conservation programs. Program improvements are needed. The most important improvements we can make to voluntary programs are:

- Increase accountability by setting explicit goals and timelines and ensuring full transparency regarding where taxpayers money is going and for what practices and systems.

- Focus most efforts in priority watersheds and work with groups of producers to take joint actions to solve pressing problems; even heroic efforts by award winning farmers will produce poor results if producers aren't working together.
- Target conservation within priority watersheds where it will do the most good to improve water quality; often only a small portion of the agricultural land in a watershed is responsible for much or most of the sediment and nutrient problems.
- Collect and disseminate conservation information we need to direct our programs effectively; we don't have the information we need to tell us what conservation practices are already in place on the landscape and how those practices are changing in response to market conditions and public policies such as biofuel subsidies and mandates.
- Build the technical services and scientific support network needed to get the job done.

If we take concerted action to accomplish the five objectives outlined above, we will see more results, more quickly.

Voluntary Efforts Are Not Enough

But even the most focused and best managed voluntary programs will not be sufficient to solve the water quality problems associated with agricultural production in Iowa. In part this is because of money. Given the financial and budget problems we are facing as a state and nation it is folly to think that massive increases in funding for voluntary programs will come our way.

Most significant, however, are the inherent weaknesses of voluntary programs to improve water quality:

- Producers who volunteer are often not the ones causing the most damage.
- Producers' priorities dominate especially if they are picking up part of the tab; producer priorities may be different than conservation program priorities.
- Designing programs that provide equal opportunity for all producers to participate becomes more important to legislators

than designing programs that wisely direct scarce funding to producers actually causing water pollution problems.

The weaknesses in voluntary programs too often result in random acts of conservation rather than the highly focused acts of conservation needed to solve water quality problems.

Strong Regulations Are Needed

Innovative regulatory frameworks can and should be devised. The Conservation Compliance provisions of the 1985 Farm Bill are the best current examples of "regulatory" framework that has produced real results: historic reductions in soil erosion across the United States. However, it is important to note that lack of enforcement by states has stalled further progress.

Regulatory frameworks should be devised primarily to drive producers, who are causing pollution, into voluntary programs. For example, a minimal setback of agricultural activities from waterbodies on hydrologically-sensitive land would create an incentive for polluting producers to enroll certain tracks of land in the continuous Conservation Reserve Program, where they can get paid to do what they otherwise would be required to do.

Rather than requiring all producers to have nutrient management plans, why not begin to phase out, through regulation, particularly risky practices, such as fall application of nitrogen or spreading of manure on frozen ground?

Finally, instead of command-and-control regulations applied to individual farmers, why couldn't we enter into performance agreements with groups of producers in small, impaired watersheds? Producers, organized through a producer group, conservation district, or drainage district, would work together to achieve explicit and measurable reductions in water pollution by some specified date. The producers themselves would come up with the plan for getting the job done and be responsible for working together to get the practices in place. Financial help could be provided up front to get things going, but failure to meet the target reductions would result in more restrictive measures.

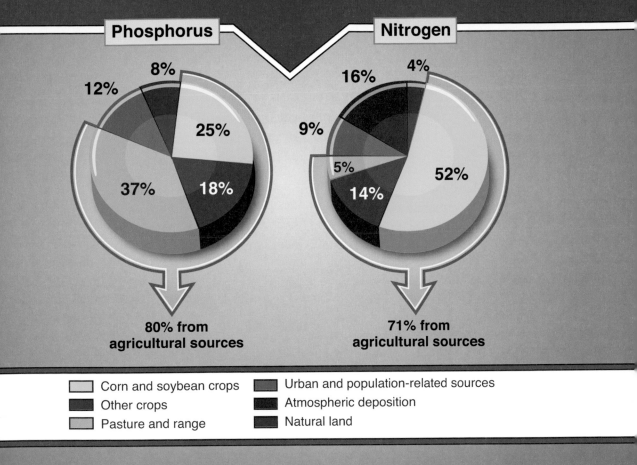

Sources of Nutrients Polluting the Gulf of Mexico

Phosphorus

8%
12%
25%
37% 18%

80% from agricultural sources

Nitrogen

4%
16%
9%
5%
14% 52%

71% from agricultural sources

Legend:
- Corn and soybean crops
- Other crops
- Pasture and range
- Urban and population-related sources
- Atmospheric deposition
- Natural land

Taken from: Environmental Working Group, "The Dead Zone Will Worsen Unless Agriculture Cleans Up," www.ewg.org/files/EWG-Dead-Zone-Factsheet.pdf, U.S. Geological Survey, January 2008.

It is time to get serious about developing regulatory programs that work—frameworks that make sense in agricultural settings and which producers can work with. These examples are a long way from fully fleshed-out proposals. But they do offer possibilities for strengthening and building on our current, voluntary programs.

TWELVE

Federal Regulations Go Too Far in Regulating Water Quality

Peyton Knight

In the following viewpoint Peyton Knight addresses the Clean Water Restoration Act (CWRA), a proposed law that would give the federal government more authority to regulate water and water pollution than it was given under the 1972 Clean Water Act. Knight contends that additional enforcement is unnecessary, because people who use the nation's waterways are already working voluntarily to avoid pollution. The new regulations proposed under the CWRA, he argues, would be especially harmful to those who hunt, fish, and engage in other outdoor recreation. This is unfair, he concludes, because outdoor sports enthusiasts have historically been protective of the environment. Knight is director of environmental and regulatory affairs for the National Center for Public Policy Research, a communications and research foundation promoting free markets, individual liberty, personal responsibility, and a strong national defense.

Congress is currently [in 2008] considering legislation that would substantially broaden the federal government's authority under the Clean Water Act. However, like many misnamed bills before it, the Clean Water Restoration Act is a lesson in false advertising. The Act would do more to threaten the cherished pastimes of hunters, fishermen and other outdoor enthusiasts than it would to ensure the cleanliness of our nation's water.

Background

For over three decades, the Clean Water Act of 1972 (CWA) has been mired in conflict and ambiguity. The Act makes it a crime to discharge pollutants into the "navigable waters of the United States" without first acquiring a federal permit. However, what began as a reasonable attempt to control water pollution in our nation's interstate rivers, lakes and streams spiraled into unreasonable federal regulation of isolated wetlands, ponds, dry lakebeds, intermittent streams and drainage ditches. . . .

[In 2008] U.S. Representative James Oberstar (D-MN) [introduced] the Clean Water Restoration Act (H.R. 2421), which he claims would "restore the authority of the Clean Water Act." Senator Russ Feingold (D-WI) introduced a companion bill (S. 1870) in the Senate.

In reality, the Clean Water Restoration Act (CWRA) does not "restore" the CWA. Instead, it greatly expands its scope and jurisdiction. The bill would bring federal oversight to activities that affect all "waters of the United States" as opposed to merely "navigable waters" as called for in the original CWA. "Waters of the United States" is broadly defined in the legislation to include "all interstate and intrastate waters and their tributaries, including lakes, rivers, streams (including intermittent streams), mudflats, sandflats, wetlands, sloughs, prairie potholes, wet meadows, playa lakes, natural ponds, and all impoundments." . . .

At first glance, the CWRA appears to advance the interests of American hunters, fishermen and other outdoor enthusiasts, given the connection between wildlife and water quality. In reality, the CWRA would threaten these interests.

Hunters: Beware the CWRA

Prairie potholes and sloughs, particularly those found in the prairie pothole region in the upper Midwest, constitute perhaps

The Prairie Pothole Region

The 300,000-square-mile Prairie Pothole Region is home to more than half of the waterfowl in North America.

The Prairie Pothole Region

Taken from: U.S. Fish and Wildlife Service, 2009. www.fws.gov/arrowwood/pothole.html.

the best duck breeding and hunting grounds in the United States. As such, in 2006 nearly 1.3 million hunters flocked to North Dakota, South Dakota, Iowa, Minnesota and Montana, the five states that comprise the prairie pothole region.

Under the Clean Water Restoration Act, however, something as simple as constructing a duck blind on private land on or near these prime hunting waters could require hunters to submit to a costly and time-consuming permitting process.

Both "prairie potholes" (depressed areas that temporarily hold rainwater and snowmelt) and "sloughs" (swampy depressions typically comprised of stagnant water or mud) are specifically named in the CWRA as "waters" that would be subject to regulation—a departure from the original Clean Water Act. As

If passed, the Clean Water Restoration Act (CWRA) would restrict the activities of duck hunters.

a consequence, driving posts into water and mud near a prairie pothole for construction of a duck blind could constitute discharging dredged or fill material into the "waters of the United States," which is illegal under the CWRA without a permit.

In addition, hunters who fire shot over and near prairie potholes, lakes, rivers, ponds and wetlands could be considered polluters under the CWRA. In 1996, a U.S. District Court in New York ruled against a shooting range when it found that expended shot, even non-toxic steel shot, is considered a pollutant under the current CWA. . . .

Fishermen and Boaters: Beware the CWRA

Like hunters, fishermen and recreational boaters would also find it more difficult to engage in their sports under the CWRA.

For example, the construction of fishing piers and boat docks, which can already require a permit under the CWA, would likely see enhanced scrutiny under the CWRA. Such construction could be regulated in nearly every instance, as nearly every body of water would qualify for federal oversight.

Though certain activities that affect navigable waters are already regulated under the current CWA, the CWRA would place even more activities under the regulatory microscope. This is because the CWRA not only broadens the jurisdiction of land and water to be regulated, but leaves it to the courts and federal regulators to determine "the fullest extent that these waters, or activities affecting these waters, are subject to the legislative power of Congress, under the Constitution." Because specific activities are not defined in the bill, all activities could be examined and potentially banned or regulated.

This means trout and small-mouth bass fishermen could lose access to their favorite rivers and streams, as wading in these waters necessarily disturbs rocks and sediment, and therefore could be considered harmful to fish and other wildlife. Lead lures, sinkers or split-shot could be deemed pollutants.

Recreational boating could be restricted or banned in certain waters due to the incidental discharge of engine cooling water, bilge water, deck runoff or ballast water. In fact, environmental litigators have already struck a blow against recreational boating under the current CWA. . . .

Shooting Sports Enthusiasts: Beware the CWRA

Already a target of the environmental movement, skeet and trap shooting ranges will likely see increased scrutiny should the CWRA become law. In fact, environmental activists have already successfully sued outdoor shooting ranges under the current CWA.

The CWA makes it illegal for anyone to discharge pollutants from any "point source" into "waters of the United States" without first obtaining a permit. A "point source" is typically a discernable source of pollution such as a factory discharge pipe. However, much like the definition of "waters of the United States," what constitutes a "point source" has been subject to broader interpretation. The EPA and courts have determined that outdoor shooting ranges loosely qualify as a "point source" of pollution into our nation's navigable waterways, and, therefore, are subject to permitting requirements under the CWA. . . .

The CWRA would create more opportunities for environmental activist groups to sue shooting ranges for Clean Water Act violations. No longer would a range's activities need to pose a threat to mere lakes and other navigable waters. An intermittent stream or nondescript drainage ditch in the vicinity of a shooting range could be sufficient ground for a crippling lawsuit.

Sportsmen Deserve Better

Though Representative Oberstar claims the Clean Water Restoration Act would simply restore the original intent of the Clean Water Act, the reality is much different. By expanding the federal government's regulatory reach beyond "navigable" waters to all "waters of the United States"—including every prairie pothole, isolated pond, wetland and intermittent stream under congressional authority—Oberstar's bill would truly enter uncharted territory. Moreover, by inviting judicial review of all "activities affecting these waters," the bill would open the door to a dizzying array of lawsuits that could challenge virtually any activity, no matter how benign, that takes place in or near any so-called "waters of the United States."

The results could be disastrous for sportsmen, our nation's frontline conservationists, who since the inception of the Sport Fish and Wildlife Restoration Programs over 75 years ago have contributed more than $10 billion for wildlife conservation efforts through excise taxes on firearms, ammunition, archery and fishing equipment. Hunters and fishermen annually provide more than 80 percent of the funding for most state fish and wildlife agencies, and in 2006 contributed over $76 billion to the economy through expenditures related to their sports.

Congress should not reward sportsmen with a measure that threatens to limit access to fishing holes and hunting grounds, and to heavily regulate or ban the use of boats, bullets, shot and tackle.

THIRTEEN

Federal Air Pollution Regulations Are Excessive

Joel Schwartz

> In the following viewpoint Joel Schwartz agrees with many environmentalists that air has gotten cleaner over the past decades, but he disagrees over whether government intervention—specifically, the Clean Air Act of 1970—is the cause. He argues that the Clean Air Act gives the federal Environmental Protection Agency (EPA) too much power, so that the EPA continues to impose unnecessary limitations on American businesses and individuals. He concludes that Congress should simplify the rules for protecting air quality and turn control of the air over to the states. Schwartz is an environmental policy researcher and consultant and coauthor with Steven F. Hayward of *Air Quality in America: A Dose of Reality on Air Pollution Levels, Trends, and Health Risks*.

The United States has achieved striking improvements in air quality during the last few decades. Between 1980 and 2006:
- fine particulate levels declined 42%;
- oxides of nitrogen decreased 41%;
- sulfur dioxide dropped 66%;
- peak ozone levels fell 30%;
- carbon monoxide diminished 75%; and
- airborne lead has been virtually eliminated—plummeting 96%.

Joel Schwartz, "Clearing the Air," *PERC Reports*, Spring 2008. Reproduced by permission.

These improvements are even more extraordinary considering that they occurred at the same time that power plants increased coal consumption more than 60 percent and the amount of driving nearly doubled. Technology—in the form of cleaner cars, cleaner power plants, cleaner paints, cleaner everything—has won the battle for clean air, even with burgeoning economic activity.

So what's the problem? The public's interest is in clean-enough air, achieved at the least possible cost. But the Clean Air Act (CAA) regulatory system is mainly about process, rather than results. The CAA and Environmental Protection Agency (EPA) regulations to implement it have created large administrative burdens, economic distortions, and perverse incentives—all of which impose costs on Americans that far exceed what is necessary to merely reduce air pollution to safe levels. Furthermore, there is no end in sight, because the CAA endows the EPA with the power to keep expanding its influence. The EPA sets national air pollution standards, so the

"Yes, son, faith can move mountains, but first you have to clear it with the E.P.A."

"'Environmental Protection Agency", cartoon by Vahan Shirvanian. www.CartoonStock.com.

agency, in effect, decides when its own job is finished. Naturally, it never will be.

Virtually everyone would agree that people have a right to be free from unreasonable risks imposed by others. But federal air pollution regulation goes well beyond this principle, and instead allows special interests—regulators, environmentalists, businesses, and politicians—to gain money, power, and prestige, and advance their ideological goals at the expense of the American people.

This article suggests a more decentralized, results-focused, and accountable approach to air quality that would guarantee clean air, but with fewer of the harmful side effects of the current system.

The Process Box

If Congress wanted states to achieve a given level of air quality, it could simply have dictated to states (1) the standards and the dates by which they would have to be achieved, (2) how compliance would be measured, and (3) the penalties for failure. Given sufficiently large penalties, states would have an incentive to find effective means of meeting their obligations. Such a Clean Air Act could be written on a few pages and would require few federal regulations.

Instead, the CAA spans hundreds of pages and includes exquisitely detailed requirements for everything from the composition of gasoline to the content of permits-to-operate for industrial facilities. The EPA has written thousands of pages of specific regulations to implement the CAA requirements, along with tens of thousands of pages of "guidance documents" to explain what the regulations mean.

States must, in turn, develop their own laws, plans, and regulations to implement the federal requirements, and businesses must obtain permits that specify operating conditions and pollution-control methods, unit by unit and process by process, and which must be amended whenever a process is changed. Legions of lawyers and consultants help regulated businesses figure out what the rules mean and how to comply with them. . . .

Conflicts of Interest

An equally damaging feature of the federal regulatory state is that it has created large bureaucracies with the authority to keep expanding their power. There is no brake built into the system.

The Environmental Protection Agency and state regulators, for public support, depend on a perception that there is still a serious problem to solve. But they are also the ones who decide when their own jobs are finished, because the EPA gets to set the pollution standards and specify the means by which the standards will be achieved. Not surprisingly, no matter how low air pollution goes, the EPA has never declared the air safe and continues to tighten the standards. The EPA is like a company that gets to decide how much of its product people must buy. Congress also charges the EPA with reporting on the costs and benefits of its own regulatory programs—like a company that gets to audit its own books. . . .

Focusing on Results

The regulatory system's conflicts of interest and blurred lines of accountability put regulators in the business of fear mongering and empire-building, rather than limiting them to the efficient pursuit of clean air. We can do better by changing our regulatory institutions to focus on results and remove incentives for bureaucratic expansion, risk exaggeration, and administrative complexity. Here is one potential option:

- Congress, not the EPA, should set ambient air pollution standards that states must attain, along with the deadlines for meeting them and the penalties for failure. States would be able to adopt more stringent standards if they wished.
- States should be on the hook only for results—that is, meeting the standards by legislated deadlines. All of the current Clean Air Act's planning, permitting, and process requirements should be removed, as should the mandates that require states to implement specific regulatory programs or approaches.

- The federal government should still be responsible for setting emission limits for a few major air pollution sources with interstate effects such as motor vehicles and power plants. As with the ambient air standards, these requirements should be chosen by Congress, rather than by regulators. Other pollution sources would be under state control and states could also go beyond federal requirements if they desire.
- The EPA's role would be limited to measuring emissions and air pollution levels and enforcing Congress's emission limits for federally regulated sources.

Some critics believe that the EPA's regulatory power should be reduced to setting emissions limits for only a few pollution sources, such as cars and power plants.

Putting legislators, rather than regulators, in charge would not be a panacea [cure-all] (Congress has imposed some foolish programs of its own, such as the ethanol mandate), but putting the onus on Congress for setting ambient pollution standards and emission limits would reduce the EPA's ability and incentive to grow its administrative empire. Legislators would have less of a stake in growing the power of the administrative state if they are directly accountable for imposing the requirements.

Environmentalists and regulators have created the appearance that the modern administrative state is a good and necessary way to protect public health. Indeed, air quality *has* improved dramatically since the 1970 passage of the modern Clean Air Act. But few realize that air quality improvements were equally dramatic in the decades *before* the Clean Air Act. Air quality is not unique in this respect. Water pollution as well as automobile and workplace safety were all improving at about the same rate in the decades before and after the creation of, respectively, the EPA, the National Highway Traffic Safety Administration, and the Occupational Safety and Health Administration.

The key difference is that before the modern era of micromanaging regulation, the government's role was complementary to market forces, evolving gradually, and largely working in concert with people's values and preferences. In contrast, today's federal regulatory system imposes revolutionary institutional changes that override people's preferences, suppress individual initiative and creativity with relentless bureaucracy, and unnecessarily curb freedom.

FOURTEEN

Fighting Pollution Is a Moral Responsibility

Jim Ball

> The following viewpoint was originally presented as testimony before the U.S. Senate Committee on the Environment and Public Works. The author, Jim Ball, explains his belief that humans are called by God to protect society's weakest members, and that this responsibility includes protecting the earth so that everyone can be healthy and safe. He argues that government figures must use both scientific and moral principles to determine, for example, how to protect children from lead, ozone, mercury, and other pollutants. He concludes that lawmakers must consider their decisions affecting pollution and climate change to be moral choices and make them wisely. Ball, an ordained minister, heads the Evangelical Environmental Network [EEN], a nonprofit educational organization that publishes *Creation Care*, a Christian environmental quarterly journal.

My name is the Rev. Jim Ball and I am President and CEO of the Evangelical Environmental Network (EEN). It is an honor to testify before you today at this hearing to review serious environmental policy concerns that have arisen in 2008. . . .

My purpose here is to offer moral guidance from a religious perspective on one of the chief responsibilities of the Senate

Jim Ball, "Made in the Image of God," Testimony before the Committee on the Environment and Public Works, U.S. Senate, September 24, 2008. Reproduced by permission of the author.

Environment and Public Works Committee, to protect the environment. . . .

How we treat both *who* or *what* is within our control, within our power, is a true test of our moral character as individuals and as a society.

How we treat *who* we have the power to help or harm is to be governed by some basic moral principles recognized by most if not all faith traditions in one form or another. These principles are that we are to:

- love our neighbors;
- do unto others as we would have them do unto us (also known as the Golden Rule), and;
- protect whom Jesus calls "the least of these" (Matthew 25), described elsewhere in Scripture as orphans, widows, and aliens or foreigners—precisely those who don't have power and are therefore vulnerable to those who do. . . .

Protecting the Most Vulnerable

When it comes to environmental concerns, how can you, as legislators, or members of the Executive Branch, as administrators, exercise power on behalf of the citizenry in keeping with the basic moral principles of loving our neighbors and protecting the most vulnerable?

You must be able to discern, first, whether something actually poses a problem, and second what is required to solve the problem.

To determine whether something poses a problem, you should rely on the best scientific evidence and analysis available. Such evidence and analysis should in turn guide you in determining what is required to solve the problem.

Take lead as an example. As the best scientific evidence demonstrates, it clearly causes harm to children, a vulnerable group within our society over whom we have power. As the most current evidence and analysis by both the EPA's [Environmental Protection Agency's] Clean Air Scientific Advisory Committee (CASAC) and the EPA's staff scientists suggests, the current

Religion and the Environment

U.S. Religious Traditions	Those who believe stricter environmental laws and regulations are worth the cost
National Total:	61%
Evangelical churches	54%
Mainline churches	64%
HIstorically black churches	52%
Catholics	60%
Mormons	55%
Orthodox	60%
Jehovah's Witnesses	60%
Other Christians	66%
Jews	77%
Muslims	69%
Buddhists	75%
Hindus	67%
Other faiths	77%
Unaffiliated	69%

Taken from: Pew Forum on Religion & Public Life, "U.S. Religious Landscape Survey," 2007.
http://religions.pewforum.org/pdf/comparison-Views+About+Environmental+Protection.pdf.

standard set in 1978 is clearly outdated and should be strengthened or improved. My hope is that when the EPA issues their final ruling in mid-October [2008] the EPA Administrator will abide by the unanimous recommendations of the EPA's own scientific panel as well as his scientific staff.

This same pattern should be followed with ozone and particulate matter.

Another air pollutant that has been clearly demonstrated to cause harm, especially to the unborn and infants and young children, is mercury. A recent estimate suggests that up to one in six babies are born with harmful levels of mercury in their blood. Yet there are still no federal protections for the vulnerable against mercury. This clearly needs to be remedied and I urge the next Congress and Administration to work together to see that this is done.

A final group of air pollutants causing serious harm to the vulnerable that is currently not regulated are greenhouse gases, particularly CO_2. On June 7, 2007, I and other religious community colleagues testified before you on the dangers climate change poses, especially to the poor, and the ethical reasons for action. The situation is even more urgent now than it was then. Given the current state of our efforts at the federal level, this represents a tremendous opportunity for the next Congress and Administration to do better.

Protecting Other Creatures

Thus far I have briefly discussed how we treat *who* we have the power to help or harm.

How we treat *what* we have under our control, including God's other creatures and the natural resources of God's Earth, is also very much wrapped up in being made in the image of God, of doing God's will. . . .

Having made us in His image, God has given us the capacity to rule over His other creatures and His Earth and the charge to rule as He would. In keeping with our moral obligations as image bearers, the Endangered Species Act (ESA) provides for the legal protection of God's other creatures within our power, helping to ensure that the blessing of life and sustenance God has given to his other creatures is not turned into a curse by us. Any diminishment of legal protection that ensures the survivability of the multitude of species created, blessed, and provided for by God runs counter to our calling to rule as God would rule. On the other hand, the improvement or enhancement of such protection is in keeping with our being made in the image of God.

Viewpoint author Jim Ball (pictured) heads the Evangelical Environmental Network, an organization of Christian environmentalists who share the belief that God intends humans to protect all creatures as well as the earth itself.

Human laws such as the ESA (or the Clean Air Act, for that matter) are not written in stone like the Ten Commandments. Certainly this law and the regulations promulgated to implement it can be improved.

For example, we must strive to do all things as efficiently as we can, in keeping with our call to be good stewards of our time and financial resources. Efficiency is good when it complements other moral goals.

But an increase in efficiency can never justify the weakening of such goals. As we have seen, another part of stewardship is the care and protection of God's other creatures to ensure that they can live the lives He intends for them. Thus, we must work to protect God's other creatures in the most efficient manner we can. . . .

The Nation's Moral Character

Thus, to be true images of God in our love and service of others, especially those within our power, as well as in our dominion or care of the rest of creation is at the core of what it means to be a moral being. Will the use of our power be characterized by service, generosity, compassion, and mercy? Or will it degenerate into selfishness, greed, and tyranny?

And so as finite creatures and Members of the Senate your exercise of legal power is tinged with eternity. You can weaken or strengthen our country's efforts to protect people, especially the most vulnerable, from air pollution and climate change. You can stand by and let others weaken them even though you have the power to stop them. You have the same moral choices concerning the protection of God's other creatures.

What You Should Know About Pollution

Air Pollution

According to an overview of the Clean Air Act published by the Competitive Enterprise Institute:

- The Clean Air Act regulates six types of air pollution: lead, ozone, carbon monoxide, sulphur dioxide, nitrogen oxides, and particulate matter. Between 1970 and 2008 emissions of these six pollutants decreased by approximately 53 percent.
- During the 1990s it cost U.S. businesses, industry, and governments approximately $21 billion each year to satisfy the requirements of the 1970 Clean Air Act. The cost is estimated to rise to $28 billion by 2010.
- Cars made in 2008 pollute about twenty-five times less than cars made in the 1970s.

The American Lung Association reports:

- Six out of ten Americans live in places where there are unhealthy levels of air pollution. Around the world, an estimated 1.5 billion people are breathing dangerously high levels of pollution every day, according to the World Health Organization.
- Members of ethnic minority groups and people with lower incomes suffer disproportionately more illness caused by air pollution.
- Secondhand smoke, or cigarette smoke inhaled by nonsmokers, is a major indoor air pollutant. It contains about four thousand chemicals, including two hundred known poisons and forty-three cancer-causing agents.

According to the Sierra Club:

- Cars and light trucks account for 20 percent of the nation's annual carbon dioxide pollution.
- One gallon of gasoline burned puts twenty-eight pounds of carbon dioxide into the atmosphere.

According to the Mercury Policy Project:

- Traditional fluorescent light tubes and newer compact fluorescent lights contain small amounts of mercury. Workers may be exposed to mercury during manufacture, transport, and disposal of these bulbs, and consumers may be exposed if the lights break.
- Approximately 670 million used fluorescent bulbs were disposed of in 2003.
- Each year broken fluorescent lights release two to four tons of mercury into the environment.

Water Pollution

A report from the U.S. Geological Survey states:

- Pesticides linger in the food chain long after they are applied. Some pesticides that have not been used for twenty to thirty years are still detected in fish and in streambed sediment at levels that pose a potential risk to human health, aquatic life, and fish-eating wildlife.

Grinning Planet, an environmental Web site, reports:

- Forty percent of American rivers are too polluted for fishing, swimming, or aquatic life.
- Forty-six percent of American lakes are too polluted for fishing, swimming, or aquatic life. In any given year about 25 percent of beaches in the United States are placed under advisories or are closed at least once because of water pollution.
- Polluted drinking water is a problem for about half of the world's population. Each year there are about 250 million cases of water-related diseases. About 5 to 10 million people die from these diseases.
- Each year plastic waste in water and coastal areas kills up to one hundred thousand marine mammals, 1 million sea birds, and countless fish.

According to the World Wildlife Federation:

- Eighty percent of the pollution in the oceans comes from land-based activities. Pollutants including oil, fertilizers, solid garbage, sewage, and toxic chemicals are dumped into the oceans or run into them from drains and rivers.
- Fertilizer runoff from farms and lawns contains nutrients that cause eutrophication, or the flourishing of algal blooms that deplete the water's dissolved oxygen and suffocate other marine life. Eutrophication has created enormous dead zones in the Gulf of Mexico, the Baltic Sea, Chesapeake Bay, and other areas.

According to a 2006 United Nations Food and Agriculture Organization report, *Livestock's Long Shadow*:

- Raising livestock for food is one of the main contributors to water pollution.
- Grazing livestock uses 30 percent of the earth's land surface. Producing feed for livestock uses 70 percent of the earth's agricultural land. Eight percent of the earth's freshwater is used for raising livestock for food.
- Thirty-seven percent of the pesticides used in the United States and 50 percent of the antibiotics are used in livestock production. Traces of these chemicals end up in rivers and streams.
- Raising livestock for food produces 65 percent of the human-induced nitrous oxide, 37 percent of the methane, and 68 percent of the ammonia—three significant air pollutants.

Electronic Waste

The U.S. Environmental Protection Agency estimates:

- Between 26 million and 37 million computers became obsolete in the United States in 2005. That same year a total of some 304 million electronic devices, including computers, cell phones, televisions, and monitors, were taken out of service in American households—two-thirds of them still in working order.
- The electronics disposed of in 2005 weighed about 1.9 million to 2.2 million tons. Most were sent to landfills; less than 400,000 tons were recycled.

- In 2007, 29.9 million desktops and 12 million laptops were discarded in the United States—about 112,000 computers each day. About 31.9 million monitors were disposed of in 2007.

According to the Electronics TakeBack Coalition:

- Over 1 billion cell phones were sold around the world in 2006. Only about 10 percent of cell phones are recycled.

Opinions About Pollution

According to March 2009 Gallup polling data:

- Americans' highest environmental concern is over pollution in drinking water. Fifty-nine percent of respondents said that they worry about pollution in drinking water "a great deal," 25 percent worry "a fair amount," and 16 percent worry "only a little or not at all."
- Fifty-two percent worry "a great deal" about pollution in rivers, lakes, and reservoirs, 31 percent worry "a fair amount," and 27 percent worry "only a little or not at all."
- Fifty-two percent worry "a great deal" about contamination of soil and water by toxic waste, 28 percent worry "a fair amount," and 19 percent worry "only a little or not at all."
- Forty-five percent worry "a great deal" about air pollution, 31 percent worry "a fair amount," and 24 percent worry "only a little or not at all."
- For each of the four concerns mentioned above, fewer people were concerned "a great deal" than in 2000, but more were concerned "a great deal" than in 2004.
- In another survey the same month, respondents were asked whether economic growth or protecting the environment should receive priority, even if the other suffers. Fifty-one percent said that economic growth should take precedence, while 42 percent favored protecting the environment. This was the first time in the twenty-five-year history of the annual survey that more respondents favored economic growth.

According to a nationwide Harris Poll from May 2008:

- Seventy-two percent of U.S. adults believe their personal actions are "significant on the environment"; twenty-two percent believe their actions are not significant.

- Women are much more likely than men to believe that their actions are significant. Seventy-seven percent of women believe that their actions are "significant on the environment," compared with 67 percent of men; 35 percent of women believe their actions are "very significant on the environment," compared with 21 percent of men who believe the same.
- Fifty-three percent of Americans say they have done something to change their lifestyle to make it more environmentally sustainable, while twenty-five percent say they have not. Of those who have made changes, 91 percent recycle, 47 percent have bought "green" household products, and 10 percent have considered becoming vegetarians or have made the change.

What You Should Do About Pollution

Many of the problems caused by pollution seem to be too big for one person to fix. Others involving large corporations or government bureaucracies and regulations seem so complicated that young people still in school cannot have much influence over them. Still, there are many ways that you can make a difference now—and ways you can position yourself to continue to make a difference later.

Pollute Less

As a student you probably are not the one in your family who decides which car, appliances, cleaning products, or even food the family buys. But with many of the things that you use yourself—from T-shirts to toilet paper to TVs—there are choices you can make to create less pollution.

The most polluting thing the typical American does every day is drive or ride in a car. By walking or riding a bike for even a few trips a week—or taking public transportation, if it is available—you can produce less air pollution, get more exercise, and save on the cost of gasoline. Other ways to reduce automobile emissions include accelerating gradually, driving the speed limit, and making sure your tires are inflated properly.

It is easy to forget that there is a power plant out there somewhere generating the electricity that it takes to run your television, computer, and chargers for your cell phone and MP3 player. These power plants, often coal burning, produce large amounts of pollution, so although the connection may not be obvious, you can pollute less by using less electricity. And since a great deal of the electricity we consume is wasted, most people can reduce their electricity use without any real hardship. It is as simple as turning off the TV when you are not watching it (and even putting the TV and DVD player on a power strip that you turn off every night), turning off lights and your computer when you are not using them, and unplugging your cell phone charger or MP3 charger unless you are actually charging something.

If you are in the habit of buying a new computer, cell phone, or MP3 player every time styles change or new features are introduced, think carefully about what you will do with your old device when you are done with it. Many cities have special electronics recycling collections to help make sure that the toxic chemicals in discarded electronics are not mishandled. Goodwill Industries, a training and education organization for people with disabilities, has a national program that accepts and recycles electronics at no cost to consumers. And many communities have agencies that accept old cell phones and distribute them to soldiers, senior citizens, and domestic violence shelters. Make sure you dispose of your old equipment responsibly.

When it is time to buy new electronics, take the time to learn which models are made with fewer toxic materials, and buy from companies that have responsible recycling programs. The Electronics TakeBack Coalition (www.electronicstakeback .com) issues an annual report evaluating the responsible practices of companies that manufacture and sell TVs, computers, cell phones, and other products. The Web site of another group, the Silicon Valley Toxics Coalition (www.etoxics.org), features an "Electronics Purchasing Guide" and an "Electronics Recycling Guide."

Finally, a note about drinking water. Many consumers believe that drinking bottled water is safer because it contains less pollution than water out of the faucet. In fact, study after study has concluded that this is generally not true. Many brands of bottled water are nothing more than municipal water drawn from a faucet straight into the bottle, and some brands actually contain more contaminants than city water (which is generally quite safe in the United States). If you like to carry water for convenience, get a reusable water bottle and keep it clean. You will be saving the pollution caused by moving water from across the country—or across the world—to your grocery store, as well as the pollution generated by making and disposing of the bottles.

Work Together

To amplify the impact of your personal choices, encourage others to reduce their own polluting activities, and seek out people who know more than you do and who can teach you new "green" tricks. Many schools sponsor environmental or ecology clubs, where students can undertake research projects together, exchange information, and take on activities to educate and involve their communities. Environmental clubs at middle schools and high schools organize school-wide recycling programs, put up posters, offer educational activities for elementary school students to teach them about pollution, write to their government representatives, or clean up local parks or streams. If your school does not have an environmental club, or if you would like some new ideas about what your club could be doing, visit the Web sites sponsored by EarthTeam (www.earthteam.net), the Greenspan Environmental Club Network (www.greenspanworld.org/environmental_club_network.htm), and the U.S. Environmental Protection Agency Student Center (www.epa.gov/students).

Outside of school, regional and national organizations are always looking for volunteers and new members. Local branches of your state's Department of Natural Resources or the Nature Conservancy and national groups, including Greenpeace, the Sierra Club, and Ducks Unlimited, conduct work days and educational workshops. And be alert for information about preventing pollution every April. Since 1970, April 22 has been observed as Earth Day, a day when local, regional, national, and international organizations sponsor volunteer opportunities and educational programs to work toward a healthy environment.

Whether you work alone or in a group, it is important to educate yourself about the issues surrounding pollution. With libraries in most schools and towns, and with the power of the Internet today, it is easier than ever to read widely, find out what different people think, reach your own conclusions, and share them with others through a blog, a social network site, a conversation in the lunchroom or at the dinner table, or a letter to your senator. Even as a young person, you can make a difference when it comes to preventing pollution.

The editors have compiled the following list of organizations concerned with the issues debated in this book. The descriptions are derived from materials provided by the organizations. All have publications or information available for interested readers. The list was compiled on the date of publication of the present volume; the information provided here may change. Be aware that many organizations take several weeks or longer to respond to queries, so allow as much time as possible.

American Coalition for Clean Coal Electricity (ACCCE)
333 John Carlyle St. S., Ste. 530
Alexandria, VA 22314
phone: (703) 684-6292
e-mail: info@cleancoalusa.org
Web site: www.cleancoalusa.org

The ACCCE is a partnership of the industries involved in producing electricity from coal. Its goal is to advance the development and deployment of advanced clean coal technologies that will produce electricity with near-zero emissions. On its Web site, the ACCCE offers background information on coal-based energy. Visitors can register for regular e-mail updates on the issues. The group also maintains another informational Web site, America's Power, at http://behindtheplug.americaspower.org.

American Enterprise Institute for Public Policy Research (AEI)
1150 Seventeenth St. NW
Washington, DC 20036
phone: (202) 862-5800
fax: (202) 862-7177
Web site: www. aei.org

The AEI is a private, nonpartisan, not-for-profit institution dedicated to research and education on issues of government, politics, economics, and social welfare. The institute's community of scholars is committed to expanding liberty, increasing individual opportunity, and strengthening free enterprise. The AEI's research group on energy and the environment has published reports, opinion pieces, and white papers, including *The Consumer Burden of a Carbon Tax on Gasoline* and *A Green Economy, or a Sea of Red Ink?*

Basel Action Network (BAN)
c/o Earth Economics
122 S. Jackson St., Ste. 320
Seattle, WA 98104
phone: (206) 652-5555
fax: (206) 652-5750
Web site: www.ban.org

BAN is the world's only organization focused on confronting what it views as the global environmental injustice and economic inefficiency of toxic trade (toxic wastes, products, and technologies) and its devastating impacts. The group actively promotes sustainable and just solutions to the consumption and waste crises, banning waste trade while promoting green, toxic free, and democratic design of consumer products. BAN's Web page gathers up-to-date e-waste news articles from a variety of international sources and offers a photo gallery, reports, speeches, and even poetry. There is also a link for finding responsible recyclers of electronic waste.

Competitive Enterprise Institute (CEI)
1899 L St. NW, 12th Fl.
Washington, DC 20036
phone: (202) 331-1010
fax: (202) 331-0640
e-mail: info@cei.org
Web site: www.cei.org

The CEI, founded in 1984, is a nonprofit public policy organization dedicated to advancing the principles of free enterprise and limited government. The CEI argues that the best solutions to environmental problems come from individuals making their own choices in a free marketplace. It publishes opinion and analysis pieces on its online *EnviroWire,* an online Daily Update, and the book *The Environmental Source,* covering global warming, free-market environmentalism, biotechnology, chemical risk, and more.

Environmental Defense Network
257 Park Ave. S.
New York, NY 10010
phone: (800) 684-3322
Web site: www.edf.org

The Environmental Defense Network, founded in 1967 to work for a ban on the pesticide known as DDT, works to protect the environmental rights of all people, including future generations, low-income communities, and communities of color. It focuses on U.S. environmental problems and the U.S. role in causing and solving environmental problems, particularly in the areas of global warming, land, water, wildlife, oceans, and health. The Environmental Defense Network maintains an online archive of its articles, reports, press releases, and fact sheets, as well as resources for educators, and allows visitors to the Web site an opportunity to register for e-mail updates.

Evangelical Environmental Network (EEN)
1655 N. Fort Myer Dr., Ste. 742
Arlington, VA 22209
phone: (703) 2248-2602
e-mail: een@creationcare.org
Web site: www.creationcare.org

The EEN is a nonprofit organization that seeks to educate, inspire, and mobilize Christians in their effort to care for God's creation, and to advocate for actions and policies that honor God and protect the environment. The EEN organizes and participates in public education and advocacy campaigns and declarations on energy and the environment, provides educational and inspirational materials and resources to individuals and churches, and publishes *Creation Care,* a Christian environmental quarterly journal.

Greenpeace

702 H St. NW, Ste. 300
Washington, DC 20001
phone: (202) 462-1177
e-mail: info@wdc.greenpeace.org
Web site: www.greenpeace.org

Greenpeace is an international nonprofit organization that accepts no funding from governments or corporations. Founded in 1971, it focuses on worldwide threats to the planet's biodiversity and environment and directs attention to its mission through public acts of nonviolent civil disobedience. Greenpeace publishes reports, including "Canned Tuna's Hidden Catch" and "Recycled Tissue and Toilet Paper Guide," and an annual *Guide to Greener Electronics*.

Grinning Planet

Web site: www.grinningplanet.com

With the slogan "Saving the Planet One Joke at a Time," this Web site combines humor with information about health, energy, and environmental issues. The site offers articles, cartoons, videos, and audio.

National Center for Public Policy Research

501 Capitol Court NE
Washington, DC 20002
phone: (202) 543-4110
fax: (202) 543-5975
e-mail: info@nationalcenter.org
Web site: www.nationalcenter.org

The National Center for Public Policy Research, founded in 1982, is a communications and research foundation dedicated to providing free market solutions to today's public policy problems. Its researchers believe that the principles of a free market, individual liberty, and personal responsibility provide the greatest hope for meeting the challenges facing the United States in the twenty-first century. The foundation sponsors the Center for Environmental and Regulatory Affairs, focusing on endangered species, forest policy, fuel economy, global warming, invasive species, nuclear policy, property rights, and smart growth.

Natural Resources Defense Council (NRDC)
40 W. Twentieth St.
New York, NY 10011
phone: (212) 727-2700
fax: (212) 727-1773
e-mail: nrdcinfo@nrdc.org
Web site: www.nrdc.org

The NRDC is an environmental action organization that works to support pro-environment legislation and defeat anti-environment legislation. Specifically, it calls on government to work with its citizens to reduce pollution, protect endangered species, and creating a sustainable way of life for humankind. The NRDC publishes a quarterly magazine, *OnEarth,* and e-mail bulletins including *Earth Action, Legislative Watch,* and *This Green Life.*

Pew Environmental Group
1200 Eighteenth St. NW, 5th Fl.
Washington, DC 20036
phone:(202) 887-8800
fax: (202) 887-8877
e-mail: info@pewtrusts.org
Web site: www.pewtrusts.org

One of the nation's largest environmental scientific and advocacy organizations, the Pew Environmental Group is a nonprofit, nonpartisan organization established to inform citizens about environmental problems and how they affect human health and quality of life. Its educational programs focus on global warming, protecting ocean life, wilderness protection, and public lands. It absorbed the work and the staff of the National Environmental Trust in 2008 and continues to offer reports, fact sheets, and press releases.

Reality Coalition
Web site: www.thisisreality.org

This Web site—and a series of television commercials—is produced by the Reality Coalition, a group that includes the League of Conservation Voters, the Natural Resources Defense Council, the National Wildlife Federation, Sierra Club, and other organizations. Through brief fact slides, a blog, and humorous videos, the site argues that "clean coal" is not clean and challenges the coal industry to change its advertising and its operations.

Sierra Club
85 Second St., 2nd Fl.
San Francisco, CA 94105
phone: (415) 977-5500
fax: (415) 977-5799
e-mail: information@sierraclub.org
Web site: www.sierraclub.org

Founded in 1892, the Sierra Club is the oldest and largest grassroots environmental organization in the United States. Its mission is to help people explore, enjoy, and protect the wild places of the earth and to promote the responsible use of the earth's ecosystems and resources. The Sierra Club publishes books, calendars, newsletters, blogs, and a bimonthly print magazine, *Sierra*. Its twice-monthly e-mail newsletter, *Sierra Club Insider*, offers environmental news, green living tips, urgent action alerts on environmental issues, and book and movie reviews.

Silicon Valley Toxics Coalition (SVTC)
760 N. First St.
San Jose, CA 95112
phone: (408) 287-6707
fax: (408) 287-6771
e-mail: svtc@svtc.org
Web site: www.etoxics.org/site/PageServer

The SVTC is an organization of high-tech workers, community members, law enforcement, emergency workers, and environmentalists engaged in research, advocacy, and grassroots organizing to promote human health and environmental justice in response to the rapid growth of the high-tech industry. It was founded in 1982 in response to the discovery of groundwater contamination throughout Silicon Valley near high-tech manufacturing facilities. Its Web site offers several free reports, including "Citizens at Risk," "Regulating Emerging Technologies in Silicon Valley and Beyond," and "Digital Dump."

Union of Concerned Scientists (UCS)

2 Brattle Sq.
Cambridge, MA 02238-9105
phone: (617) 547-5552
fax: (617) 864-9405
Web site: www.ucsusa.org

The UCS is an independent nonprofit alliance of concerned citizens and scientists, founded in 1969 by faculty members and students at the Massachusetts Institute of Technology who were concerned about the misuse of science and technology in society. It sponsors the Sound Science Initiative, through which scientists provide information on environmental science to government and the media. The UCS publishes an annual report and posts on its Web site information about the global environment, clean vehicles, clean energy, and other issues. It also publishes periodicals, including the e-mail newsletter *Greentips: Environmental Ideas in Action*.

U.S. Environmental Protection Agency (EPA)

Office of Solid Waste (5305P)
1200 Pennsylvania Ave. NW
Washington, DC 20460
Web site: www.epa.gov/p2

Established in 1970, the EPA leads the nation's environmental science, research, education, and assessment efforts. The EPA maintains a page dedicated to pollution prevention (P2) on its Web site, offering basic information about modifying production processes, promoting the use of nontoxic or less-toxic substances, implementing conservation techniques, and reusing materials rather than putting them into the waste stream. The site includes databases and reports, links to local and regional contacts and laws, and a pollution prevention information clearinghouse, with fact sheets, case studies, documents, pamphlets, and posters.

Worldwatch Institute
1776 Massachusetts Ave. NW
Washington, DC 20036-1904
phone: (202) 452-1999
fax: (202) 296-7365
e-mail: worldwatch@worldwatch.org
Web site: www.worldwatch.org

Worldwatch Institute is a research institution that analyzes and focuses attention on global problems, including environmental issues such as global warming, and on the relationship between trade and the environment. It publishes annual book-length reports, *State of the World* and *Vital Signs*, the bimonthly *World Watch* magazine, and a series of *Worldwatch Papers* on current environmental topics. The Web site also offers Eye on Earth, a news service offering key developments in international environmental news.

BIBLIOGRAPHY

Books

Michelle Allsop, *Oceans in Peril: Protecting Marine Biodiversity.* Washington, DC: Worldwatch Institute, 2007.

Elizabeth Brubaker et al., *A Breath of Fresh Air: The State of Environmental Policy in Canada.* Vancouver, BC: Fraser Institute, 2008.

Robert Bryce, *Gusher of Lies: The Dangerous Delusion of "Energy Independence."* New York: PublicAffairs, 2008.

Ronnie Greene, *Night Fire: Big Oil, Poison Air, and Margie Richard's Fight to Save Her Town.* New York: Amistad/HarperCollins, 2008.

Joy Horowitz, *Parts per Million: The Poisoning of Beverly Hills High School.* New York: Viking, 2007.

Chip Jacobs and William J. Kelly, *Smogtown: The Lung-Burning History of Pollution in Los Angeles.* Woodstock, NY: Overlook, 2008.

David Michaels, *Doubt Is Their Product: How Industry's Assault on Science Threatens Your Health.* New York: Oxford University Press, 2008.

Robert D. Morris, *The Blue Death: Disease, Disaster and the Water We Drink.* New York: HarperCollins, 2007.

Chad Pregracke and Jeff Barrow, *From the Bottom Up: One Man's Crusade to Clean America's Rivers.* Washington, DC: National Geographic, 2007.

Jill Potvin Schoff, *Green-up Your Cleanup.* Upper Saddle River, NJ: Creative Homeowner, 2008.

Joel M. Schwartz and Steven F. Hayward, *Air Quality in America: A Dose of Reality on Air Pollution Levels, Trends, and Health Risks.* Washington, DC: AEI, 2007.

Loretta Schwartz-Nobel, *Poisoned Nation: Pollution, Greed, and the Rise of Deadly Epidemics.* New York: St. Martin's, 2007.

Philip Shabecoff and Alice Shabecoff, *Poisoned Profits: The Toxic Assault on Our Children.* New York: Random House, 2008.

Rick Smolan et al., *Blue Planet Run: The Race to Provide Safe Drinking Water to the World*. San Rafael, CA: Earth Aware Editions/Against All Odds Productions, 2007.

Periodicals and Internet Sources

Anne Butterfield, "Coal Pollution: Hiding in Plain Sight," *Boulder (CO) Daily-Camera*, January 11, 2009.

Arian Campo-Flores, "Toxic Tsunami," *Newsweek*, July 18, 2009.

Dina Cappiello, "Toxic Coal Ash Piling Up in Ponds in 32 States," *USA Today*, January 9, 2009.

Dan Collyns, "Peru Tribe Battles Oil Giant over Pollution," BBC News, March 24, 2008.

Shaila Dewan, "Hundreds of Coal Ash Dumps Lack Regulation," *New York Times*, January 7, 2009.

Jeff Donn, "Bottled Water Has Pollutants, Too," *Huffington Post*, October 15, 2008. www.huffingtonpost.com.

Paul Driessen, "Saving Lives with Coal," *Townhall.com*, January 3, 2009. www.townhall.com.

Economist, "A Sea of Troubles: The Oceans," January 3, 2009.

Juliet Eilperin, "EPA Lets Electronic Waste Flow Freely, GAO Report Says," *Washington Post*, September 17, 2008.

Douglas Fischer, "The Dirty Side of Clean Coal," *Scientific American*, December 9, 2008.

Fort Worth (TX) Star-Telegram, "U.S. Should Not Give Up on Clean Coal," March 17, 2009.

Kent Garber, "EPA's Efforts to Curb Air Pollution in Limbo," *U.S. News & World Report*, December 10, 2008.

Louise Gray, "Pollution 'Could Kill as Many as Climate Change' Warns Met Office," *Daily Telegraph* (UK), December 6, 2008.

Kenneth P. Green, "The Worst Option on Greenhouse Gas," *American*, February 25, 2009.

Elizabeth Grossman, "Poison Ice," *Salon*. April 30, 2008. www.salon.com.

Tom Henry, "Pollution Is a Crime That Alters Lives," *Toledo (OH) Blade*, July 26, 2009.

Diane Katz, "Air Pollution Deaths Wildly Exaggerated," *Financial Post*, August 16, 2008.

————, "The Facts Contradict Environmental Alarmism," *Vancouver Sun* (Canada), May 1, 2008.

Andreas Lorenz and Wieland Wagner, "China's Boom and Doom," *Der Spiegel* (Germany), February 12, 2007.

Abraham Lustgarten, "The Hidden Danger of Gas Drilling," *BusinessWeek*, November 28, 2008.

G. Jeffrey MacDonald, "Don't Recycle 'E-waste' with Haste, Activists Warn," *USA Today*, July 6, 2008.

Blake Morrison and Brad Heath, "EPA Lists Schools for Air Checks," *USA Today*, March 31, 2009.

Veronika Oleksyn, "Cosmic Cleanup or Duck and Cover? How to Deal with Space Pollution," *Huffington Post*, February 19, 2009. www/huffingtonpost.com.

Doyle Rice, "Your Eyes Aren't Deceiving You: Skies Are Dimmer," *USA Today*, March 13, 2009.

Sacramento (CA) Bee, "Time to Back Off on New Fuel Nozzle Rule," March 31, 2009.

Space Daily, "Americans Owe Five Months of Their Lives to Cleaner Air," January 25, 2009. www.spacedaily.com.

Peter N. Spotts, "Midwest's Postflood Risk: Toxic Basements," *Christian Science Monitor*, June 30, 2008.

John Vidal, "Health Risks of Shipping Pollution Have Been 'Underestimated,'" *Guardian* (UK), April 9, 2009.

Claudia Wallis, "Study Links Exposure to Pollution with Lower IQ," *Time*, July 23, 2009.

Bryan Walsh, "E-waste Not," *Time*, January 8, 2009.

————, "Exposing the Myth of Clean Coal Power," *Time*, January 10, 2009.

Melanie Warner, "Is America Ready to Quit Coal?" *New York Times*, February 15, 2009.

Jeanne Yacoubou, "The Vegetarian Solution to Water Pollution," *Vegetarian Journal*, January–March, 2009.

INDEX

PICTURE CREDITS